Get That Job!

-

Pissing People Off
One Email at a Time

Anthony C. Alcamo

Get That Job! Pissing People Off One Email at a Time
Copyright © 2012 Anthony C. Alcamo, gofurther corporation

ISBN-13 (paperback)   978-0-9854918-0-2
ISBN-13 (electronic)   978-0-9854918-1-9

Printed and bound in the United States of America.

First Edition: June 2012
10 9 8 7 6 5 4 3 2 1

For my family.

Patricia, Cole, Annalia and Michael.
Group Hug - Goooooooooooo Alcamo's!

Preface

I have been a software architect and developer for over 20 years. I sincerely enjoy the information technology industry and most of the work I have performed. During the first decade of my career, I held 7 different fulltime jobs, and over the next decade, I had 10 different consulting assignments at various companies. Before leaving a job or when the end of an assignment drew near, it was necessary for me to send my resume and many emails to both employers and recruiters. I collected, maintained, and amassed thousands of these email addresses (mostly for recruiters). Since its inception, this list has grown to well over 50,000 unique email addresses.

This process worked well and kept me employed for most of my career, but over the past several years, many of these recruiters have started playing a similar 'numbers' game. Most of the solicitations I have been receiving are for positions not applicable for my skill set or inappropriate location. Initially, I would reply to many of them, explaining why the opportunity was not viable for me, or that I would not relocate (which is clearly indicated on all job boards that I subscribe to). This did not work, however, and without removing me from their distribution lists, or changing their search attributes in their system, I would continue to receive irrelevant job opportunities emailed to me. This frustrated me for a long time... until I decided on a different approach.

Instead of explaining my job criteria to these boneheads, or requesting that they kindly remove me from their distribution, I began to have a bit of fun with them. This book contains those emails where I insult, degrade, and mock these 'trained' idiots, and I was rather surprised to find out how persistent (and clueless) they actually are. Do they like being called a dickweed? Don't they update their database with my correct information?

Amazingly, they continue to contact me, hoping I will entertain their next job offering with at half my current pay or work 3,000 miles from my home. Sounds perfect - where do I sign?

I suppose I must be doing something right, however, since my inbox is full of job opportunities from more recruiters in a day than most of my friends get in a month, and some are actually viable. That's when I decided to document my strategy for the benefit of others.

Introduction

With the downturn in our economy and the staggering number of people looking for work, this book will show you how to get the perfect job for yourself using some unconventional methods. These methods are shown by example, in the form of various emails chains between me (the instigator) and recruiters (idiots).

Warning: Many of these advanced job-seeking techniques I help you employ are intended for the sophisticated reader. Consequently this book will use strong language such as ballbag, bitch, and ass-clown. In **addition, adult concepts including Rusty Trombone and Dirty Sanchez have been used to help communicate and clarify ideas to the recruiter.**

With very few exceptions, I will allow each email conversation to play out completely, guiding the recruiter into the most ridiculous scenarios. I will not stop the conversation unless:

- The recruiter catches on and has a good sense of humor.
- The beating has taken its course, and is no longer funny.
- I feel terrible about what I have done (this has not yet occurred).

The content of these emails have not been altered with the exception of some spelling and punctuation for clarity, and some omissions for brevity. Many of these recruiters use fragmented sentences and poor spelling, which have not been altered in an attempt to preserve the true essence of their emails.

Also, each email has been 'turned upside-down' so the reader can read it in conversational form rather than reading from the end to the beginning as emails are generally formatted.

Some of my recipients had a good sense of humor, others not so much; several are still waiting for me to send them my updated resume or even friend them on a social network site, lol. Good luck with that!

Below are the conventions used throughout this book.

Responses	All of my responses are *italicized*.
[bullshit]	Areas denoting unnecessary information are bracketed.
{actions}	Actions are denoted within curly brackets.
------------	Personal information has been omitted to protect the stupid.

Some final notes about information exchange:

When a recruiter asks me to provide them with personal information, I simply reply with a bunch of crap to appease them and continue the process. I give them fake phone numbers, social security numbers, basically everything I tell them is bullshit.

Whenever a recruiter asks me to attach my current resume, I either attach nothing or attach some binary file on my machine, after renaming it resume.doc. Recruiters don't understand this advanced renaming process, and simply find that they cannot open the resume – it must be their computer. They grow even more confused when they cannot locate the 'missing' resume.

Did I upset many of these recruiters? You bet I did! But sometimes, we must sacrifice the feelings of a few for the good of the majority. Put differently, I had the best time shitting all over them. I laughed out loud, and you will too – now let's begin!

Table of Contents

x

Communication

Communicate Effectively

I cannot emphasize how critical effective communication is when speaking with a recruiter. Just as the recruiter prides himself or herself on using clear, concise language when describing a job opportunity or the many nomenclatures associated therein, so should be your goal as well.

Each recruiter will have his or own unique style. There are times in which you should adapt to their style, and times which you should 'pave your own road'. The tools I provide you in this section will help you navigate the recruiter's many styles of communication, and help you decide which style to adopt in order to be most effective.

Subject:	Direct client requirement for Java developer - Portland, OR - Long Term
Sender:	Annu
Date:	28.11.2011
Background:	My German boss runs around the office in his underwear waving a gun.

Hi,

This is Annu from ------ Solutions. Our direct client has a requirement for the position listed below. Please contact us if you are interested with this requirement.

[required skills]

Thanks and regards

Annu -----

----- Solutions Inc

(512) --- ----

Annu,

I am very interested in this project, however, I have a boss who is a big bully and constantly watching me - what can I send you to get started?

Thanks,

Anthony

Please send me your resume copy and your contact details to proceed further.

Thanks and Regards

Annu

Annu,

My resume is attached. I can only communicate via email until my boss leaves the office to go to the firing range. Can you let me know the culture at your client's site please?

Thanks,

Anthony

{attached fake resume}

HI ANDREY,
Please fill the form given below and the attachment without missing any information. Here the client is ---. We are working directly to them. You have to take two levels of technical interview. First round will be telephonic. And the next round will be a webcam interview or videoconferencing. I can arrange the interview before this evening. Please let me know if you have any questions.

[form]

Thanks and Regards
Annu

Annu,
I am comfortable with both types of interview (phone and webcam). I'll call you the moment my boss leaves. He's wearing his shooting glasses in the office right now (I guess to intimidate everyone). He knows we all need our jobs real bad, but if he ever pulled out a Glock or Colt Single-Action I would just grab my ham sandwich and run. Anything else I email you in the meanwhile?
Thanks,
Anthony

[Annu lists all the questions again]

Annu,
All (most) of the necessary information is below, inline.
My boss is now running around in his boxers (shooting glasses still on), shouting German stuff. He even spit on my friend. When can you set up the first phone interview?
Thanks,
Anthony

Hi,
Can I call you now?
Thanks and Regards
Annu

Annu,
If I unlock the bathroom door, he's gonna get me. This has
happened before. I just gotta let him chill out for a while. Can I
contact you later (as soon as he goes shooting)?
Thanks,
Anthony

Subject:	Fulltime position for J2EE Architect in Cupertino, CA
Sender:	Rahul
Date:	16.02.2012
Background:	Rahul has an anger issue – Ted to the rescue!

Dear Anthony
Our records show that you are an experienced IT professional with experience relevant to one of our current open position. Please let us know whether you would wish to evaluate one of the open positions we have with our customer based out of Cupertino, CA. My firm -------- Technologies Inc. is headquartered in California and provides nationwide staffing support to our client.
[skills and responsibilities]
Regards,
Rahul -----
Great Results. Always
Direct: (408) --- ----
Milpitas, CA 95035

What's up jerky?
Do you know the rate on a 1099 or c2c basis?
Peace out.

I am fine, what about you moron?
This is a fulltime position.
Rahul

Are you familiar with the location dickweed?

YO its mentioned in the subject line dickhead.
Rahul

Then you are a complete asshole as I live 3000 miles from there, lol. You have got to be the stupidest recruiter ever - what a joke you are. Good luck with your 'career', lol lol

Buzz off...... you don't deserve a job...... Wish you get unemployed soon.

Listen up ballbag - although you are not worthy, I will give you some advice. When engaging in witty banter, you must seek council, as you are simply inadequate. I will refrain from commenting on your grammatical errors to save you some embarrassment. Now please look like you are busy so you are not replaced with a monkey of equal (or better) talent.

Why don't you mid your own business......
Rahul

Only if you apologize immediately and refer to me as your 'Super-Duper Leader'

Get lost

Say it, bitch.

I googled a bit about your company and found its one man street shop. You must be the owner of the company, who actually doesn't have any work which in-fact is very frustrating. And after understanding your situation I give you a piece of advice-please consult a psychiatrist you poor frustrated bastard. And one more thing call your mother a bitch.
Rahul

I am your master. You know it. Say it bitch.

Freaking Buzz off, master my shit.

You do not understand, grasshopper.

8

You must bow before me and lick ballsack.

You are just a waste cocksucker
Rahul

[I gave him a day to think about it]

Good morning my little bitch.
You must have given this much thought and come to your
senses. I anticipate an apology and then you lick my asshole.
Your master awaits.

Hey guy do some work......

Do you agree that you are not a good recruiter?
Your master awaits.

Moreover you know nothing about recruitments, I have a logic
reason for sending that email. And anyways if you have received
and email is this the way you respond to it. Why are you so
desperate to get yourself called as a master? End it up I have
some serious business to do.

This sounds like an apology for wasting my time.
I did not however see the term 'Master' in the body.
You are now given another opportunity to reform.
Say it bitch.

I tried calling you and heard your voicemail message, you don't
sound like a kid. Why are you behaving like a kid?

focus grasshopper, I am trying to help you.
now say I am your master, bitch.

You are shit you eat shit and you speak shit...... so you son of a
bitch fuck off and don't send me an email. Ask your mom to beg
me to fuck her......... you weirdo.

I am blocking your emails, so that I don't see your fucking name again in my inbox. Hey bastard.... yes I am addressing you...... yes you son of a bitch...... ha hahahahahahahaha

{I create a fake email account (Ted) and pretend he is my boss}

Ted,
I did not start this - this guy started harassing me.
Anthony

Rahul,
Good afternoon. My name is Ted and I am Anthony's boss. It has been brought to my attention that some disturbing emails have been sent to you by Anthony. Please accept my deepest apologies for this behavior. Would you please explain to me how this started?
Thank you,
Ted Kowalski

Hi Ted,
This all started because I found his profile on one of the job boards and I sent him an job opening via email. I know that the requirement was in California and he lives in eastern zone. But I just took a chance may be he would be interested for the opportunity? As you have the chain of emails below you can just see that he firstly addressed me as jerky and then it all happened? During all the email exchanges I tried cooling him couple of times but this guy kept on abusing and the joke is that he wants himself to be called as master. Lastly I just wanted to say that I have blocked him from sending any email to me and I tried calling him on the number mentioned on the website but he didn't responded. Let's finish it off and I am blocking your company domain as spam. I appreciate your email and concern, hope we have no hard feelings.

Rahul,
No hard feelings at all.

*I must say, however, that you are the stupidest fucking recruiter
ever! There's no Ted you asshole - this is Anthony, your master,
LOL! How much time did you spend on this email you idiot?
I hope you have learned a lesson here grasshopper.
Now bow down before me.
Your master,
Anthony*

Subject:	Hi Please go through the Java requirement its Contract to Hire position!!!
Sender:	Phani
Date:	15.02.2012
Background:	I call Phani names until he doesn't like me anymore. By the way, my name is T-Bone.

Hi,
Good afternoon, Here is a C2H (contract to hire) position for Java Please go through the full job description please go through the requirement and let me know if you are available and your interest in forwarding your resume for this position so that we can close the position. Local to Reston, VA
[job details]
Thanks & Regards
Phani -----
----- Infotech Inc.
Voice: (732) --- ----

What's up douche?
My resume is attached.
Please confirm.
Thanks,
TBone

{attached fake resume}

Hi TBone
Resume sent by you is not opening there is some problem with the format can you please send the resume once again please in another format.
Thanks & Regards
PHANI

Alright, calm down ass clown.
I saved is as word 97-2003 and attached the file here.

Please let me know if this works.
T-Bone

{attached second fake resume}

Sorry not even this time it is showing as file corrupted can you
please send it PDF format
Thanks & Regards
PHANI

I think I see the problem you bone smuggler.
I've converted the file to pdf and attached here.
This should work - let's connect tomorrow.
T-Bone

{attached third fake resume}

{I wait a day for Phani to respond}

Phani,
Good morning shaboinka,
I did not hear back from you and assume the file was good.
Please let me know either skin pole.
Thanks,
T-Bone

Subject:	Sr.Java Architect - fulltime/Permanent - Cupertino - CA - US
Sender:	Swapnil (Swapi)
Date:	07.12.2011
Background:	Shnookums has no idea what the conversation is really about. I think he even once refers to me as Johnny. Ironically, this position requires excellent communication skills.

Hi Anthony,
Good Morning,
Hope you are doing great..!!
I have a urgent opening for my client for Sr. Java Architect role please let me know your interest and availability ASAP – Please do send me your updated resume in a word format ASAP
CLIENT: ------- Technologies.
[job requirements]
Excellent Communications skills

Thanks & regards
Swapnil
Recruiting & Staffing Consultant
P: (801) --- ----
Murray, Utah 84107

Hi Swapi.
Do you know how many people work there?
Thanks,
Anthony

Hi Anthony,
Thanks for your reply, can you please let me know what exactly you want to know regarding how many architects work or total number of people (Employees) work in the company..??

14

Please let me know - waiting for your reply. Also please do send me your updated resume in a word format, so we can go ahead for further process..
Thanks & Regards,
Swapnil

Let's do this one beefcake.
Do you have my resume?

Yes i do have your resume and please find the attached copy of your resume and let me know if that is the updated profile. Also please send me few information below from your end ASAP

[requested information]

Waiting for your reply ASAP
Thanks & Regards,
Swapnil

Aforementioned is attached twinkle-toes.
Please contact me with any questions you may have.
Thanks.

{attached fake resume}

Hi Johnny,
Good Morning, Thanks for your reply - Can you please fill in the details and send back to me ASAP:-

[candidate details]

Thanks & Regards
Swapni

I have never been interviewed by ------- Technologies, pookie.
Also, do I need a Visa specifically, or may I use Discover?
Thank you,

Anthony

Hi Anthony,
Please let me know the required information below which is really mandatory to submit to the client. I tried calling you couple of times and left you voicemail –Can you please give me a call ASAP And please fill the details below and send back to me..

[candidate details]

Thanks & Regards,
Swapnil

I will try to answer each of these in order, shnookums.
Can you extract the other information from my resume?
How soon: 2 weeks
Visa: no - US citizen

Sure i will take other information from your resume. I would wait for your reply - Actually its pretty much delayed now-I need to submit your profile to the client ASAP. Rest info i have with me. Waiting for your reply at the earliest
Thanks & Regards,
Swapnil

Here is the rest of my info big-daddy-yum-yum.
Wanna meet at a lollipop-stop, then go for a drink?

{provided fake details}

Hi Anthony,
Project requires to Relocate to Cupertino, CA - so please let me know your comfortable part regarding relocation. If you are not willing to relocate then client wont consider, because project in based in CA and candidate needs to relocate for the position. Waiting for your reply ASAP.

[Swapi brings up the issue of location after wasting my time]

I would consider relocating to Cupertino, but not if you're hung like a tic-tac.

Hi Anthony,
Can you please let me know your contact number wanted to talk to you for few minutes, so we can go ahead for further process of submission to the client -------..Please share me your contact details ASAP
Thanks & Regards,
Swapnil

This is too easy, ButterCup, let me move on to another issue: Are there ample apartments that are pet-friendly in the area? I have 2 gerbils, squibbles and puff-puff that I will not leave behind.

Frankly speaking I am actually not aware about the exact area in cupertion, CA where it is pet friendly area. So i request you that once you get the project in CA, you can take look into nearby areas and find the pet friendly environment, because I am really not aware of the place. I am also really concerned about your pets - because I am also having a Labrador retriever who is just 8 months old and i know regarding the shifting of pets. Please let me know how you would prefer and go ahead for further process and schedule your interview with the client. Waiting for your reply ASAP.
Thanks & Regards
Swapnil

Can you send me a picture of your dog so I can add it to my screensaver?

I have sent you a request on Facebook you can check it - i have in my profile.

Hi Anthony,
We have an urgent requirement for a J2EE Developer. This is a
Full Time position based in Richmond, VA.
[job details]
Thanks and look forward working with you.
Regards,
Soujanya -----
-------------- LLC
Phone : (732) --- ----
North Brunswick, NJ 08902.

You are very kind Soujanya..
My resume is attached.
Also, please let me know if I am pronouncing your name
correctly.
Thanks.

Hi Anthony,
Could you please attach resume.
Thanks & Regards,
SOUJI

I apologize. Is it pronounced Souji or Souji?
In either case, my resume is attached.
Thanks,
Anthony

{attached fake resume}

18

Hi Anthony,
We are not able to open you resume. Could you please cut paste your resume are resend in word document.
Thanks & Regards,
SOUJI

Still not sure if I'm pronouncing it correctly - does it sound like sushi? Anyway, I took my resume, did a cut (windows ctrl-x), but how do I paste it into an email?

My name you can pronounce it as Souji.
Just do cntrl c and Paste it in the Email thats it.
Thanks & Regards,
SOUJI

Ok, thank you shortbread.
I tried to paste it, but strange characters appear in the window. Do you have any other suggestions?

send you resume in note pad.
Thanks & Regards,
SOUJI

Will do. Do you want me to send it overnight or is two-day ok?

Send it by tomorrow.
Thanks & Regards,
SOUJI

Cool. I'll send it to suite 203. Do you want me to have the signature waived or will you be in the office?

Subject:	Immediate Interviews: Urgent opening for Sr. Java/ J2EE Developer : Alpharetta, GA 30009 / Warren, NJ 07059
Sender:	Sumit
Date:	29.11.2011
Background:	Fluency in multiple languages can often be an asset. Sumit respects me because I know how to speak jive.

Hi Anthony,
I am SUMIT ------, Technical Recruiter with ------- CONSULTING INC. We have a Contract opportunity with one of our Fortune 500 global telecommunications company major clients, located in WARREN, NJ 07059 / ALPHARETTA,GA 30009.(MULTIPLE POSITIONS ON BOTH LOCATION).
[job details]
Warm regards,
SUMIT ------
------- CONSULTING, INC.
Office: (770) --- ----

sup mofo. I gots da good. Does ya have my resume?

No I don't have, Please send me your resume and best time to reach you so we can discuss in details.

Shyot biatch, you cants grab it off da dice o monsta?
let me know, and Ill emails a copy to ya if not.

Yes I got your resume, please call me to discuss in details about this position you can reach me at 770-255-3570
Thanks
Sumit

y'all be havin any forms dats I gots a complete?
can y'all send dat shyot over ta me?

[page of requirements]

wat da hell is all dat krap for?
is it all nessissary?
y would y'll need my visa anyway?

Hi Anthony,
First of all we need these details if you want to pursue this
opportunity and we don't need your visa, we require your work
authorization in USA. Let me know if you are interested.
Thanks
Sumit

Shyeet sumit, I'z thawt you wuz wack - i'm down dawg, aight?!
I see now we'z tight - b4, I thawtyou'z after my yayo.
can I send it to you l8r? I'z got to jet wit my hottie.
Peace yo

Subject:	Java Developer--Multiple Positions for project at San Antonio, TX
Sender:	Anil
Date:	21.11.2011
Background:	I recon Anil is two sandwiches short of a picnic.

Hi,
We are JAVA DEVELOPER--MULTIPLE POSITIONS FORPROJECT AT San Antonio ,TX. SEND QUALIFIED RESUMES TO ANIL.-----@------.COM
[job details]
Thanks & Regards
Anil
IT recruiter
Phone: (510) --- ----

Howdy Anil!
Let's talk turkey - what's the rate?

Hi,
The client is offering the best rate like50$/hr. If it is okay for you lease send me your updated resume. I am looking forward to your reply...Thank you

Well I say, that sure is a big bag of beans!!
Do you offer medical, dental, that crap?

Hi,
The client is offering all the inclusive 50$/hr

I say I suppose if was to work 11 or more hours per day, that'll be enough to fill my 10-gallon hat in less'n a weeks time. Do you reckon?

Okay,

but the client is mentioned only duration. They didn't mention any time period per a day...

Well, right now I'm busier than a set of jumper cables at a redneck picnic. Ya mind if I email my resume in a bit?

Hi,
please send me your updated resume ASAP. So, that we can proceed further details....I am looking forward to your reply.

Anil, has the butter slipped off yer noodle? I'm fixin' to high tail it, dawggonnit, it's just that I been busier than a one-legged man at a butt-kicking contest. Can y'all jest not have a hissy-fit?

Ask Many Questions

Many potential candidates feel awkward about asking too many questions. They sometimes feel that they can be an annoyance to the recruiter, driving them away, and possibly ruining their chances of a job opportunity.

This is, in fact, the furthest from the truth! Recruiters will respect you more if you ask them many questions about the opportunity they are presenting. They may even hold you with higher regard if you should ask them ancillary questions, completely unrelated to the job position.
Do not be afraid to ask as many questions as possible!

No question should be considered stupid or inappropriate, and recruiters will respect your desire to know more about the prospective client. They are always happy to help you find the next most compelling and fulfilling role in your career path. Remember, the recruiter is there for you, not unlike a close friend you might invite to your home for the holidays.

Hi,
My client is looking for C++ ARCHITECT for FULL TIME
EMPLOYMENT ii OMAHA NE. If you are interested, please send
me your updated resume ASAP with below details:
[job details]
Thanks and regards,
Gulzar -----
Phone #: (480) --- ----
----- LLC
Tempe AZ 85284

Gulzar,
I am interested in this job if you are interested in me.
Thanks.

Hello Sir,
Please send me your resume with below details,

[list of details]

Thanks and regards,
Gulzar

Gulzar,
I'm sorry - I don't understand.
Are you interested in me?
Thanks

I need to check your resume first, please send me your resume
Thanks and regards,
Gulzar

No problem - I understand. My resume is attached.
You need to check me out before I might be considered.
It's kinda like when those judges at the dog show force the dog's
mouth open to check its teeth and squeeze their balls before
they watch them run around and jump through the hoops.
Let me know what you think.

{attached fake resume}

Subject:	Urgent need for Senior Java J2EE Developer at Stamford, CT
Sender:	Ajay
Date:	22.02.2012
Background:	Make certain you understand the requirements.

Hello,

Hope you are doing great.

This is Ajay --------- from --------- Technical Resourcing. --------- TECHNICAL RESOURCING IS NOW THE 4TH LARGEST IT STAFFING FIRMINTHE WORLD besides [others omitted]. We are directly working with most of BIG 50 CLIENTS. We have an urgent requirement for SENIOR JAVA J2EE DEVELOPER at STAMFORD, CT and in search for a good match I come across to your resume. So wanted to know, whether you are available or looking for any kind of job change

[job description]

Thanks & Regards,

Ajay -----

Technical Sourcing Recruiter

Direct: (781) --- ----

Ajay,

I noticed this in the job description: "Must be a fast learner and ready to work in a fast paced, dynamic environment." Would you please elaborate a bit on this?

Thanks,

Anthony

Words are simple and the client is Starwood Hotels and they want a quick learner because if the consultant is not from their industry background then he must learn fast and their environment is fast paced and dynamic.

Thanks & Regards,

Ajay

Got it Ajay!
I just wanted to make sure these people aren't running around
like crazy through the halls, etc.
My resume is attached; please let me know.
Thanks,
Anthony

{attached fake resume}

Anthony,
Your resume is not opening can you resend me your resume
again and also please provide me the below details:

[job details]

Thanks & Regards,
Ajay

Sure Ajay, but would you please speak to this requirement first:
"Reviews project requests with Development lead, PMO Lead,
Security & Application/Infrastructure Architecture teams." I just
want to make sure I understand their need before I throw my
hat in the ring.
Thanks,
Anthony

These are simple Developers responsibilities which developer
has to do on regular basis...
Thanks & Regards,
Ajay

Thank you Ajay, although that wasn't the level of detail I was
looking for. Anyway, what's this one about: "These solutions
must be aligned with business, IT strategies and comply with
overall architecture standards."
Thanks,
Anthony

Sorry Anthony,
I am a recruiter not a developer and if you want to know these things then I am sorry to say that you are not even a Junior developer who also use to handle these responsibilities at a lower level. So now until you share your profile along with the below details with me, I can't answer your any questions.
Thanks & Regards,
Ajay

Ajay,
I am appalled that you would infer my talents are below that of a junior developer. I will have you know that I have architected some of the most highly-available, scalable, fault-tolerant systems in existence today. My first objective is to simply understand the client's needs and assure a strong alignment with my background, skills and such. Do you understand?
Thanks,
Anthony

Then check my first line I am a recruiter not a developer... I just search the skills matching with the required skills and more or less the responsibilities are same... that's all a recruiter can do... If you want to know about the client I can tell you and I already told you the client name is -------- Hotels... So you can also check about the client online as they are very big client in Hotel Industry. And one by one you are asking about the responsibilities... can't you ask all of them at once, Also my contact number is given below, you can directly call me and ask me about all the things since the morning we are playing emails - emails. This position is hot and client is moving fast and I am not the only one who is searching the consultants, there are many more recruiters are also trying for same piece of sweet.
Thanks & Regards,
Ajay

Ajay,

I am not sure what you mean by:"...there are many more recruiters are also trying for same piece of sweet."
Anthony

I mean there are many more recruiters who are also searching consultant for this same position and if the client will choose their consultant for the position then I can lose this position from my hand.
Thanks & Regards,
Ajay

Ajay,
I think I understand - but who are the other recruiters?

Hello Anthony,
Would you like to apply for this position or not?
Thanks & Regards,
Ajay

yes I do, please.

Please provide me your updated resume and below details to complete the submission process:

[job details]

Thanks & Regards,
Ajay

Ajay, What does "Visa Status" mean?

Visa Status means what is your work status in US, Like you are a US Citizen or Green Card Holder of you have any other working permits like H1B or TN or EAD...
Thanks & Regards,
Ajay

Thank you Ajay. I don't have a cell phone - what is a landline?

Ha hahaha funny... lol zzz :)
Thanks & Regards,
Ajay

Hi,

Hope you are doing well. I am a Staffing Specialist for ------ Solutions, a global company specializing in staffing both Consulting and Full Time positions. If you are interested in the opportunity listed below, please forward your updated resume along with current contact information, or perhaps you can recommend someone who would be interested in this position. [job details]

Thank you very much for your time.

Prem -----

------ Solutions

(201) --- ----

Good afternoon Prem, and thank you.
I am interested, and have the skills necessary.
I was wondering - does the client offer educational assistance?
Thanks

Hi Antony,

What is your hourly rate on W2. What is the best time to reach on phone?.

Thank you,

Prem

Market rate is fine.
Do they offer educational assistance?

Hi Anthony,

This is contract to hire position. So, when project goes to fulltime, client will give assistance. As of now no educational assistance.
Thank you,
Prem

Ok, thanks. I know it's a bit premature, but I am almost completed my pilot certification - do you think they might reimburse me for the remaining aviation courses?
Thanks,
Anthony

Hi Anthony,
They will only do it when you goes into permanent position.
Thank you,
Prem

Very cool. So they will pay for my courses to obtain a pilot's license, right? This is very important.

Hi Anthony,
It's a contract to hire position and client will not pay until project turns to fulltime. IF they have reimburse policy only then they will pay. At this point we are unsure of whether they will Reimburse or not.
Thank you,
Prem

I am very interested, but now a bit hesitant. Do you think this tightness of the purse strings is a precursor to further expenses (travel, books, escort services, etc)?

Hi Anthony,
IF they have reimburse policy only then they will pay. At this point we are unsure of whether they will Reimburse or not.
Thank you,
Prem

I understand Prem - you're saying that they DO reimburse, you are just not sure WHAT they reimburse, correct? Next, I would like to highlight on my resume the areas of expertise most interested by your client. Would you please let me know what they are?

Hi Anthony,
Yes. That's correct.
Rate: $50-$52/hr on W2 without benefits.
Thank you,
Prem

Thank you. What would it be with benefits?

At preset you will be hired on contract (without benefits) later on fulltime/permanent (with benefits).
Thank you,
Prem

This is a bit confusing - I would start as a consultant, right?

Yes.
Thank you,
Prem

Got it, thank you. What is my start date?

Start & End date: 11/28/2011 to 03/23/2012
Thank you,
Prem

Perfect - who should I ask for when I arrive?

What is your Phone Number?.
Thank you,
Prem

Here's the thing Prem - where I am currently working, mobile phones are not permitted and everyone has a desk on their phone, but they all go through the 'trunk' via a single line (in essence, we all share a single line). If someone sees me make a call or receive a call, they will secretly listen to my conversation and tell my boss. Is there anything that you need prior to my start date?

Subject:	Position open for Java System Engineer in Boston, MA (Strongly recommended) or Charlotte, NC
Sender:	Pooja
Date:	17.11.2011
Background:	Can my dog Miku ride the train with me?

Hello Anthony,
We have following position open. Please let me know if you are interested.
[job details]
With Warm Regards,
Pooja -----
----- Inc.
Sunnyvale, CA 94086
Phone: (408) --- ----

are there buses nearby?

Yes..public transport is available between Cold Spring Harbor to Boston, MA on regular basis. Please suggest.
With Warm Regards,
Pooja

great! can you confirm that mta allows pets?

MBTA allows Dogs.
With Warm Regards,
Pooja

Thank you - that helps.
He (Miku) is about 42 pounds - will this be too large?

I would suggest you to check MTA guidelines or call customer care. Iam not having fair idea about it.:(
With Warm Regards,

Pooja

Miku actually bit someone on a bus once, but no formal documentation was filed. Anyway, I'm sure I can leave him with my Aunt Martha – she also has a dog and they get along quite well. Let's discuss dress code for a moment - is this place business casual?

Yes...the position is with Bank ---------- and they have business casuals dress code.
With Warm Regards,
Pooja

Cool, because I have a closet full of Hawaiian shirts. That wouldn't be considered too ethic, would it?

It should be proper formal.
With Warm Regards,
Pooja

Not a problem at all. Miku chewed my last pair of flip-flops last week anyway, lol. Do you know if they have a cafeteria on-site, or would I need to go out for lunch each day.

Here is the Google view nearby client location. Please have a look. I am in Sunnyvale and not having the actual idea of it. This is the best I can figure it out for you. If you need more info you can also try to get this info on google map.
With Warm Regards,
Pooja

Almost looks like Disneyland - should be fun!!
Who should I ask for when I arrive tomorrow?
Also, can you recommend a dentist in the area?

Subject:	Colorado anyone? Sr Java SW Engineer positions near DENVER for your review
Sender:	Jonathan
Date:	18.11.2011
Background:	How's the reception down there?

Hello I am an IT Recruiter. My client is a Global Financial Information Technology leader and they are looking for a in their Lakewood, Co office. Your information came up in my search and I thought that you would be interested. Please take a look at the description below and let me know what you think.
[job details]
Thank you
Jonathan -----
Sr Managing Recruiter
----- Staffing Solutions
T: (212) --- ----
C: (917) --- ----

how close to the Grand Canyon?

Same state! Its near denver
Jonathan

Can I get WI-FI when I'm in the canyon?

thanks for the laughs!
Jonathan

Jonathan, have a great weekend and Thanksgiving!
Anthony

you too. Thanks Anthony
Jonathan

Presentation

Proper Appearance

What may seem obvious or very straightforward to some people seems to elude many job seekers on their quest for a new job. Wearing your best suit after a thorough shower and shave just might give you the edge you need over a similarly qualified candidate.

It can be helpful to know the dress code of the client prior to an interview to prepare just the proper attire with which to make your first impression. Having the 'inside scoop', the recruiter will be able to provide you with the client's dress code requirements.

Subject:	Immediate Opening for Java Developer at Dallas, TX. ***Fulltime***
Sender:	Ramya
Date:	29.11.2011
Background:	What are the preferred undergarments?

Hi Anthony,
We have a Fulltime position and was wondering if you are interested. The job description is below. Please let me know if you are comfortable with the requirement. Please send me your resume, contact details and rate info and we can discuss additional info. Thanks.
[job details]
Thanks & Regards,
Ramya
Technical Recruiter
----- Solutions, Inc.
Office (972) --- ----

What is the dress code there? I am allowed to wear a hat and boots at my current employer's place.

Thank you so much for your reply. The dress code is formals. Hats and boots are not allowed for this position. Please let me know your thoughts!
Best Regards,
Ramya

Ramya,
My resume is attached.
As far as undergarments, what is your preference?
Thanks,
Anthony

{attached fake resume}

44

Yeah, I even think so. Can you please send me your updated resume so that we can discuss further regarding this position?
Best Regards,
Ramya

sounds like these snobs are a bit uptight considering I always wear socks under the boots. after working there for several months, I'm sure there would be some leeway - your thoughts Ramya?

Dear Consultant,
We have the following opening with my direct client. If you are interested and meet all of the requirements, please email me a word resume and I will contact you.
[job details and requirements]
Web Services (SOAP and REST)
Surya -----
Sr. Recruiter
----- Resources
Ph: (404) --- ----

Surya, this sounds promising - when are they looking to bring someone aboard?

Hi Anthony,
Thank you for your response. The start date would be 2-3 weeks from now. Please let me know f you are interested.
Regards,
Surya

I am, and I am EXCELLENT with SOAP and REST!!!

Anthony,
Please send me your updated resume ASAP and let me know your salary expectations.
Regards
Surya

everyday, I shower, then take a 2-hour nap.

46

No problem i will wait for your response and please find the attached screening details form.
Regards
Surya

Got it Surya, thanks! Do you need this information right away, or can I take my shower and nap first?

Sorry to disturb you but its take hardly 2mins of your time. Please send it to me ASAP.
Regards
Surya

ok, no problem - I'll just do a quick hand-wash (you know, under the pits and balls, etc), and I'll fill it out and send it to you. Will you be able to reply when you get it?

Sure will do.
Regards
Surya

I just realized (after finishing my balls) that I deleted your email with the form. would you be kind enough to resend it to me? I'll wash my pits in the meanwhile.

Here you go..

Quick question:
On the form where it specifies 'Candidate', is this me or you?

Candidate means you...

means I what??

Anthony,
Did you get chance to fill the screening form?
Regards

Surya

You have perfect timing Surya, I just awoke from my nap. Like I said, I was not sure what you meant by 'Candidate means you...'. I thought maybe it meant 'Candidate means you have to do something...'. I gotta hit the head - would you please be more specific.
Thanks!

No need of screening form will take that information you're your profile. Please send me your updated resume and expectation Salary..
Regards
Surya

You are very kind Surya. I will fill it out the best I can. Just let me finish waxing my upper thighs and I'll send you both this form and my resume. Would you like me to send it via mail or email?

By email..

I think I sent it Surya, but check the attachment - I might have accidentally attached an incorrect document which contains the names and numbers of people I tagged (banged) plus, and you'll love this – a wallet-size photo of my sack. Anyway, would you please check if you got
the right email?

I didn't receive any attachment from you.

That blows. This is becoming very frustrating - every time I click the paperclip, another browser instance opens to www.chickswithdicks.com. Sounds like a virus - what happens when you click the paperclip?

48

Subject:	Direct Client Urgent Need for Java Web Developer (Inpersonal Interview)
Sender:	Avinesh
Date:	24.02.2012
Background:	Dress for success and put your best foot forward.

Hi All,
Hope you are doing well. Please find the job description and
Send me Matching profile along with the below details.
[job details]
Thanks & Regards,
Avinesh -----
----- Global Technologies Inc.
Newark, DE 19702
Direct: (302) --- ----

Avinesh,
I noticed in your subject, that this is an 'inpersonal' interview – is
this correct?
Thanks,
Anthony

Yes they are asking for a in personal.
Thanks
Avinesh

What should I wear?

Nothing

So just hang my briefcase from the ol' dick?

Leadership and Other Valuable Skills

Leadership is the cornerstone of the successful individual. Most of the greatest leaders I have had the pleasure to meet radiate of an intrinsic motivation, most useful for speaking with dumb-ass recruiters.

These out-of-box type thinkers continually adapt and try new (and possibly untested) managerial techniques. Over years, they remain flexible and expand their sphere of comfort.

Subject:	Excellent opportunity for Java tech lead with ---- --- .
Sender:	Nihar
Date:	22.02.2012
Background:	Unconventional management techniques.

Dear Anthony,

Please have a look on the below opportunity. I would like to submit you for this position. This is with ----------- bank. If you find it interesting, Please send me your updated resume. This position is for a senior tech lead with expertise in leading the Web applications for data services in Enterprise ---------- Group. The primary responsibility of the Master Application Developer is to lead the technical design and development of cross-functional, multi-platform application systems, and will need to provide functional, technical, and/or process leadership.
[required skills]
Thanks & Regards,
Nihar -----
----- Consulting, Inc.
Office: (804) --- ----
Cell: (804) --- ----

Nihar,
Thank you for the consideration.
I believe I am quite qualified for this role. I have successfully led many teams and mentored many developers. I further believe in maintaining a common vision and an open work environment. Now how many of these monkeys would be reporting to me?
Thanks,
Anthony

Thanks Anthony for reply. You will be heading 5-6 persons there. May i know your expected hourly rate, Please also attach your latest copy of resume.

Regards,
Nihar

Thank you Nihar.
I am open to a fair market rate. How are these monkeys
currently kept in line? If they have behavioral issues, I've got a
stick I use. I tried to attach a resume, but your server denied it.
What would you like me to do?
Thanks,
Anthony

Please can you send me the resume at my gmail id ---------
@gmail.com
Regards,
Nihar

I attached my resume here Nihar.
As far as the 5-6 monkeys on this team, have you ever tried
ballgags? Shock treatment has been substantially proven over
the recent years as well. Please confirm that you received this
email, and that HR is ok with stun guns.
Thanks,
Anthony

{attached fake resume}

You are really jolly person. Thanks for the resume. But I cannot
open this file here as well. I think the problem is from your end.

Thanks Nihar.
I pride myself on being jolly, but firm when necessary. Such is
the case when I've got to kick some ass on these monkeys.
Cattle prods and whips are not beyond the scope for some of
em. Please try the attached resume. I converted it to Word 97.
Thanks,
Anthony

Thanks Anthony i got the resume now. The best houly rate for this role would be $66/hr on W2. Please let me know if this is acceptable to you.

Nihar,
I am confirming the rate of $66/hr. Of course a good salary is always beneficial, but it is most important for me to continue growing my interpersonal and managerial skills. During my last assignment, I instituted many motivational campaigns, such as the "Please don't feed the developers" artwork, and modernized cages complete with electric feedback. Also, if you have any pictures of these freaks, please email them me. Will you be able to send my resume to the client today?
Thanks,
Anthony

Thanks Anthony. Next to this mail i am going to send you two more mails regarding the submission. Please have a look on those mails and revert me back.
Regards,
Nihar

Nihar,
I got your emails. And wanted to know if I should confirm to that email or this one. I can't wait to start whipping these bitches. Gonna friggin' tie 'em all up together and piss on 'em to start with. Wake up bitches, it's golden shower time!!
Thanks,
Anthony

Anthony you need to confirm the RTR mail and need to fill the details on another mail.
Regards,
Nihar

Nihar,

I think I understand. Do you need it faxed or is email acceptable? I'll bring my mace, spurs, pepper spray, and dog collars to start. These freaks are gonna know how baby calves feel before they're veal chops.
Thanks,
Anthony

Email is acceptable Anthony.
Regards,
Nihar

Oh shit, I just reread this Nihar.
I already sent the info to you in a package that should arrive by Friday. Listen, when you get it, I need my tazer gun back - could you send it back to me? I want to try some chemicals on those freaks before I start the shock therapy. Do you need me to get you any info faster than that?
Thanks,
Anthony

Subject:	Please confrim..............NEED YOUR QUICK REPLY........ INTERVIEW SCHEDULE....Please tell me which slot are you okay for the INTERVIEW.....
Sender:	Surya
Date:	07.12.2011
Background:	Surya ferrets an interview schedule.

Hi ALCAMO,
Good Afternoon. Hope you are doing great. Well I submitted you to the client ----------- on 29th NOV...I have a interview schedule.... I got 3 slots for you.. Can you please tell me which slot is okay for you so that I can set up the interview with the Client manager.. Also please confirm that you will be available at the mobile number given. Date:Wednesday 12/7/11 8:30am-10:00am CST Thursday 12/8/11 8:30am-10:00am CST Friday 12/9/11 8:30-10:00am CST Job Title: Java Developer 3 – LB
Thanks & Regards,
SURYA ------
(248) --- ----
------- SYSTEMS INC

ok

you okay for the INTERVIEW.....

yes please.

Hi ALACAMO,
If you confirm on which date and time, you are comfortable I will update it to the client manager and I shall tell you who will be calling you and so on..so please hurry up.....
Thanks & Regards,
SURYA

{I did not respond}

Hi ANTHONY,
Good morning. yesterday I sent you many emails asking you for a correct date ,time of the below mentioned 3 days so that I can setup an interview.. I didn't get a proper reply. I guess you are busy. I even called the number I was given and I was being told you are not available and at home. This is of very high importance, I appreciate your quick reply, so that I can fix the interview. Of the 3 dates given below please tell me when you are ready to take up the interview and please tell me at what number you will be available for the interview...

Date:Wednesday 12/7/11 8:30am-10:00am CST
Thursday 12/8/11 8:30am-10:00am CST
Friday 12/9/11 8:30-10:00am CST

Sorry I have been so busy.
Tuesday will be fine.
Thanks

Hi Anthony,
The interview schedule is on today, tomorrow and on Friday...Please tell me whether you can take up an interview on tomorrow or on Friday at the timings given below.....
Thanks & Regards,
SURYA

Surya, hold on a minute - TODAY IS TUESDAY!!!
I think I missed the opportunity - why didn't you tell me??

Hi Anthony,
Don't worry,,,, I have been trying to reach you since 2 days, you aren't reachable over phone. please check all my emails...Today is Wednesday....you have interview again tomorrow and on Friday, tell me when you can take up the interview...
Thanks & Regards,
SURYA

My whole week is now screwed!
I already postponed my surgery (which was supposed to be today) to wait by the phone. As far as Wednesday, am I supposed to now switch my tae-bo class again?? Hugo will be pissed! Let me see if my mom can come over and watch the ferrets on Friday maybe I can do it then. What times work on Friday?

Phi NATHONY,
Shall I set the INTERVIEW on Friday... Friday 12/9/11 8:30-10:00amCST....please confirm...
Thanks & Regards,
SURYA

Surya,
Friday's gonna be a bust on account of my mom can't watch the friggin' ferrets. These g0ddam furry rats have blown so many opportunities for me - not just this interview either. I was once getting a handjob when one of these fur-mongrels scared the crap out of this ho so bad she jumped out of the tub and hit her face on the toilet - what a mess (not to mention I had to finish myself off). Can we reschedule for next week possibly?
Thanks,
Anthony

58

Hi Anthony,

My name is Aniket----- and I'm with ---- x Inc. (---) in Richmond, VA. --- is an International IT Consulting firm specializing in providing elite technical talent to our prestigious national client base on a consulting basis. I am interested in speaking with you and would like to know your availability and desired career direction. Details of the opportunity are provided below, and I would really appreciate it if you can send me your updated resumes if interested. I look forward to speaking with you very soon.

[job details]

ANIKET

SR. TECHNICAL RECRUITER - STAFFING SOLUTIONS

OFFICE: (804) --- ----

RICHMOND, VIRGINIA 23220

Good morning Aniket.
I am very motivated this morning.
Do you have a copy of my resume?
Thanks,
Anthony

Hi Anthony,

Thanks for your response.

Attach this resume of yours I have with me. Please let me know is this your updated word copy of resume and please let me know best time to reach you to discuss about the position.

Thanks & Regards,

Aniket

Aniket,
This resume is a bit out of date - I will attach an updated one
here. Do you know why I am so motivated? I have intrinsic
motivation, which comes from within oneself. It is based upon
concepts such as autonomy and the striving for mastery in one's
endeavors. I also got head in the shower this morning.
Thank you,
Anthony

{attached fake resume}

Hi Anthony,
I am not able to open your resume. Can you please send me doc
file of your resume.
Thanks & Regards,
Aniket

{attached second fake resume}

Aniket,
I converted it to pdf format and attached it here.
Have you ever gotten head in the shower? Handjob, etc?
Thanks,
Anthony

Greetings,

My name is AJAY and I'm an IT recruiter at --- CONSULTING,INC. Our records show that you are an experienced IT professional with experience relevant to one of my current contract openings. The job is located in GEORGIA with one of our Fortune 500 Direct client. Following is a more detailed description of the job. If interested and available, please reply with your updated MSWord resume and details given below -
[job details]

Thanks & Regards,

Ajay -----

------- Consulting Inc.

Phone: (770) --- ----

Ajay,
When are they looking to fill this spot?

Hi,

A very good morning to you ! As per the client information, they are interested to start the project as soon as possible. If you are available to join this project, please reply with your updated resume and details -

[list of questions]

Thanks & Regards,
Ajay

And a superblifent morning to you as well!
I can start one week from today. Thank you.

Hi,
Thanks for your prompt reply to me. Please reply back with
following details and your most updated resume.
Thanks & Regards,
Ajay

Ajay,
Answers are inline/below.
Magnorifcally,
Anthony

Hi Anthony,
I need your contact number and current location with city and
state name. Also please do let me know what is the rate (on
hourly basis on W2) you are looking for this position.
Thanks & Regards,
Ajay

Ajay,
Phones are down (I'm accessing a hotspot from another office,
superglorifically). I am open to market rate.
Thanks

Hi Anthony,

Below you will see a description for a Java Developer position I currently have available. It is located in Fairfield County, CT and is a permanent full time position. If you or anyone you know are interested in this role, please feel free to contact me. The developer will own their projects for the entire lifecycle.

Mission Critical applications that affect the flow of the business. They will work directly with the business user understanding the requirements, develop, test, implement and support the application. Must have 7 years in development of Java applications. Excellent oral and written communications skills [job details]

Thank you,

David -----

Recruiting Specialist

-----, a division of ----- Global Resources

Westport, CT 06880

(203) --- ---- Direct

(203) --- ---- cell

How flexible is the client?

What flexibility are you looking for?

How long and far can they bend over while I bill them?

Be a Team Player

It is just not enough to be competent at one's discipline. You must be able to work well with others in order to realize a greater synergy. Often it is difficult to convey the possession of this attribute to the lowly recruiter. I have found it helpful to express this by example, taking the recruiter down a myriad of scenarios.

Subject:	Java Developer -North Miami, FL-6 to 12 months contract
Sender:	Ramanatha
Date:	02.02.2012
Background:	Why am I on Ramanatha's distribution list? I have no idea, but I play along because I am a true team player.

This may be a quick win... commercial client Please let me know if you have a suitable consultant available for the following position. Please submit a copy of the resume, a completed copy of the skill sheet and your rate requirements.
[jobs details]
Ramanatha ------
ramanatha@-------.com
(469) --- ----

Ramantha,
I may have a suitable candidate. She's not very good looking, but an excellent Java developer.
Please let me know if this could work.
Thanks,
Anthony

We need skilled working developer and good in technically and why should care about her looks and other things?
Ramanatha

I totally agree, it's just that this one's got small tits and missing several teeth. If your client can look past that, I'm sure you could get her for a discounted rate.
Let me know.

Send resume with rate?
What is her current location?

66

Her resume is attached. Her breath ain't so bad, but she cannot take off her shoes at the client site.
Thanks

{attached fake resume}

unable to open the resume. send resume in ms word -97 format and also let me know her current location

I've converted it to Word-97 and attached it. Just keep in mind that this freak farts like all the time, everywhere! She is willing to relocate, however.
Let me know.

Subject:	Need- SAP PP/DS
Sender:	Sai
Date:	2.11.2011
Background:	This is one of my favorites! My friend, Ishmatal loves it also!

Hi,

Hope you are doing great, I have an Opportunity for you below if you are interested Please respond back me with your updated resume and the expected pay rate.

POSITION: SAP PP/DS

DURATION: 1+MONTHS

LOCATION: BROOKVILLE, PA

[job details]

Thanks & regards

Sreevatsav

------ Corporation

Schaumburg, IL 60173.

Phone: (847) --- ----

Sai,
How many openings do they have?

Hi,

We have only one opening for this position. Could you please send me your updated resume, I have forwarded you the job description from my mailing list, sorry for not having your resume.

Is it possible that if I secure this position, I could fire someone and bring my friend in?

Hi,

I am sorry, but I did not get what you were asking. Could you please elaborate what you wanted to ask

Here's the situation Sai. My roommate will not come with me unless there is work for him as well. With your help, my plan would be to receive acceptance to this position, then shortly after, I could have someone that reported to me terminated (don't worry, I'll find a cause). Then you submit my roommate's resume to me, I hire him, you make some bucks, my roommate is happy, and all is good. Are we cool?

Yeah we are cool. Could you please send me your resume. May I know what is your visa status? And can you tell me what is your excepted pay rate? And I would prefer calling me sree.

As far as the rate, market rate is fine. I am a US citizen and my friend is from Kyrgyzstan (but please keep this to yourself as I brought him here and he does not have any papers - he does have his shots, though, so it's cool). How soon might you be able to set up an interview?

First I have to show your resume to my Manager, that's why I am asking you to send your resume. Could you please send it

Ok, let me rework it a bit to emphasize the areas that your client requires. On another note - you are gonna love Ishtumal (my roommate). What a pisser - this guy can actually eat glass. Please let me know if you would like me to highlight any of my specific skills.

Hi,
Could you please send your updated resume that you said you wil l send me. On Friday I left the office so could not reply to mail.

Sai,
I'm still reworking my resume. Ishtumal and myself both worked at the same place for a while, and I wanted to remove that reference so we could execute our plan. Not important, but it was the Blue Oyster Bar in the red-light district. Anyway, I'm

going to change it to Wells Fargo or something and submit it to you. Is there a particular time you need this by?

Yeah by tomorrow the position closes. And am already holding two resumes for this one position and my manager is going on asking what is the status of the requirement. So, if you send me the resume as soon as possible I could submit yours or else I would have to go with the resumes which am having.

Dude, seriously throw those other ones away. Me and this glass-eater are gonna make you rich. We talented in many ways and know how to 'work the system'. Also, set up an off-shore bank account if you don't already have one.
Thanks.

Okay, dude will be waiting for your resume but make it as soon as possible. So, that I don't get into trouble in my office.

If they give you a hard time, I will send some of Ishtumal's friends there to 'talk' to them. No one's gonna give you a hard time when they got there not-sack in a vice - nuff said, bro?

Actually I work from India dude, so that's the problem right. And I have sent you a request from my yahoo account add me up. And could you tell me your name

Sai,
It's Anthony - I thought I mentioned that earlier. My head's been a bit fuzzy - Ishtumal has been driving me crazy - wants me to walk him day and night, always peeing on the carpet, etc. If we get this gig, I'll be able to afford some depends and a ball-gag for him.

Okay sure Anthony. But make fast dude. And add me up in yahoo also.

70

Sai, Ishtumal just did the funniest thing - he took the rubber end off of a plunger, put it in his mouth, and suck the stick up his butt!!! It looks like it goes right through him - he's now dancing like that on our kitchen table - I have to send you pictures, lol!!!!

Lol's What a funny guy?

Sorry this is so late - there is no wi-fi in the hospital. Ishtumal fell off the table onto our glass blown elephant collection - what a mess, not to mention poor Ish. I'll get back to you asap.

Hey, did you finish working on the resume???

Finally arrived home. Ishtumal's catscan proved negative (the nurses joked that they did an elephant-scan). Anyway, just cleaning, reassembling the plunger and about to make some grilled cheese. Gonna sprinkle a little 'sleepy' powder on Ish's so he can get some rest. I'll send it in a bit - are you working today?

Yeah am working dude. And good to hear that he fine now.

OMG - I JUST GAVE ISHTUMAL A GORILLA MASK - I am not kidding, I can barely type I'm laughing so hard - wait till he wakes up!!! He's gonna go crazy sick like at that last Freddie Mercury show when we gave him too many Cosmos and he started dancing on stage in that peacock outfit!! I'll touch base later.

Subject:	Availability List
Sender:	Suchi
Date:	16.02.2012
Background:	Suchi has mistaken me for one of his recruiter friends. I am thrilled to be included in his distribution, and enjoy participating using various 'alias' names.

HI,GREETINGS.....KINDLY LET ME KNOW IF YOU HAVE ANY REQUIREMENTS. YOU CAN REACH ME ON 972--------- EXT: 214OR SEND AN EMAIL TO BELOW IS THE AVAILABLE LIST OF CONSULTANTS

NAME	TECHNOLOGY	EXP (YEARS)	AVAILABILITY	CURRENT LOCATION	PREFERRED LOCATION
BEN	BA	6	IMMEDIATE	IL	OPEN
SETH	ANDROID DEV	4.5YRS	2WEEKS	GA	NY/NJ/CA
SIMIT	COGNOS	7	IMMEDIATE	DALLAS,TX	OPEN
SATISH	QA	7+	IMMEDIATE	PA	OPEN
VERA	JAVA	10YRS	2WEEKS	NYC	NYC
VEENA	.NET DEV	6YRS	IMMEDIATE	NJ	NY/NJ
NATARAJ	SHAREPOINT	10YRS	IMMEDIATE	DALLAS	DALLAS
SANDY	DATASTAGE	7+	IMMEDIATE	DALLAS,TX	OPEN
SIDDHARTH	COGNOS DEV	7YRS	IMMEDIATE	TEXAS	OPEN
SUBHASH	.NET DEV	7YRS	IMMEDIATE	MN	OPEN

Thanks,
kindly let me know! Looking forward to work with you!
Best Regards
Suchi
-------- Solutions, LLC.
Direct: (214) --- ----

How much would it cost for both Vera and Sandy (at the same time)? Do you have a 'rate' chart or such?
Thanks,
Harry Ballsack

72

Vera at 75/hr to 80/hr
Sandy at 45/hr
Please let me know!
Thanks
Looking forward to work with you!
Suchi

Thank you Suchi,
Thank you for your quick reply - these rates are very reasonable.
Will they be able to perform special tasks such as Rusty
Trombone or Dirty Sanchez, etc? Also, what is their availability?
Thanks,
Harry P. Ness

Discussing Personal Issues Carefully

Skeletons in the closet – we all have them to some extent, and you are not alone. There are ways to discuss these issues with the recruiter in a gentle, open manner. Recruiters are generally good-natured persons who will empathize with your particular circumstances. Be completely upfront with them, as they will help put any of your state of affairs in the best possible light for the potential client.

Greetings
I am currently looking for WEBSPHERE PORTAL ARCHITECT needed for a high profile client. Please send a WORD COPY of your updated resume if you are interested
[job details]
ASHLEY -----
SENIOR TECHNICAL RECRUITER
----- TECHNICAL TALENT
PHONE: (603) --- ----

Ashley,
I will be available in 3 weeks - is this ok?
Thanks,
Khan Vhict

Hi Khan,
It should work. Pls mail your updated word resume.

Ashley,
My resume is attached. It may be possible for me to get out in 2 weeks. I will know shortly.
Thanks,
Khan Vhict

{attached fake resume}

Hi Khan,
I am unable to open the attachment.

Ashley,

76

I have converted it to pdf - see if this works. Also, good news - the warden is going to let me out in 2 weeks if I behave.
Thanks,
Khan Vhict

{attached second fake resume}

Hi Khan,
For some reasons even this isn't opening. Can you copy paste your resume in the body of the email pls?

Ashley,
I'm going to try to convert it Word 97 format - are you using a PC or Mac? They only give us PCs in the prison, which I get to use each Tues and Thurs. Bright side is that there have been no reported rapes in the computer lab.
Thanks,
Khan Vhict

{attached third fake resume}

Hi Khan,
I use a PC. Also would you be able to help me understand the reason you are held in prison. I might need this information as I might have to share this information with the client.

Ashley,
It's a long story, but suffice it to say that I simply went to the bank to take some of my own money out. I did not know that the bank was closed, and after the cops ran me down, their detective claims I took much more than my account had at the time. If you need the report, I can ask one of the correction officers to email it to you. Let me know.
Thanks,
Khan Vhict

That's fine Khan. Pls check if you can mail your updated word resume at the earliest.

Ashley,
I asked my buddy Lube to convert it, and attached the file here.
The officer said that he will email you the report (but it's gonna
cost me). Also, I should mention that it was NOT my gun nor
explosives. Please let me know if you can read this one.
Thank you,
Khan Vhict

{attached fourth fake resume}

Subject:	Java Web Developer needed for 18 month contract in Minneapolis MN – 45635
Sender:	Charles (Chuck)
Date:	28.11.2011
Background:	I know a guy who makes problems 'go away'.

Greetings,

We have a resume on file for you as a potential candidate for an opening with our client. Details are below for your review. If this opportunity is of interest please let me know a good time to discuss and I can give you a call.

[job details]

Sincerely,

Chuck -----

Technical Recruiter

----- Technical Resources

t: (602) --- ----

sup chuck?
what kind of boss would I report to?
I don't go for that looking over my shoulder crap.

This is a senior level position and the overall manager is looking for candidates don't need hand holding so not so much of over the shoulder stuff. What is your rate?

Chuck

that's cool - I brought this small knife to my last place, and the guy was all like 'that knife's dangerous' and 'someone's gonna get hurt'. yeah, someone got hurl alright (as soon as he left the parking lot).market rate is fine (80-90/hr c2c). are there any forms you need me to complete?

Thanks Anthony,

Unfortunately the manager's budget isn't as high as we wish it would be. The max we have on this on a C2C would be $67.

Nowhere near what you are looking for. If I have anything in you range come up I can let you know.
Chuck

chuck, wait - I can do it for $65/hr. what do you need from me?

Ok, figured with your 80-90hr C2C the rate would be too low. Can you send me a current Word formatted resume? Also, this position is with Wells Fargo. Have you had your resume submitted to then for anything lately? They require an authorization form for submittal so I have attached it here. If you could complete and email it back to me with the resume that would be good.
Chuck

chuck, are they set on performing a background check?

They do require a criminal background check and a fingerprinting before being able to start.
Chuck

I'll be up front with you, Chuck, we might have a problem. Few years back I accidentally shot a guy in the supermarket (just went in for some beer and Stuffer's Pepperoni French Bread Pizza, which wasn't even that good). Anyway, they caught up with me, and the rest is history. I know I can do this job, but I'll need your help - you in?

Unfortunately if you have anything on the record the bank will not start the contract. Sorry but it's their rules.
Chuck

chuck, I just spoke with a guy - this incident will no longer come up in a background check. I have attached a set of fingerprints you can send to the client as well. will they require a drug test, or this is sufficient for me to get started?

Curious on how you can speak with a guy and then all the sudden it would not come up on a criminal background check? Also, the bank would setup a fresh fingerprinting.
Chuck

chuck, I am not at liberty to discuss the details. suffice to say, these type of 'arrangements' occur all the time. if they need fresh prints, I can make that happen - let me know.

Subject:	Java Developer needed in West Des Moines, IA
Sender:	Jon
Date:	17.11.2011
Background:	Will they perform a background check?

Greetings,
My name is Jon and I'm a recruiter at --------- Technical
Resourcing. Our records show that you are an experienced
professional with experience in JAVA DEVELOPMENT. This
experience is relevant to one of my current openings. The
position is located in WEST DES MOINES, IA
[job details]
Sincerely yours,
Jon -----
Minneapolis, MN 55402
(612) --- ----
----- Technical Resourcing

Hi Jon.
Would you please tell me how large this company is?

The company is --------
Jon

Will they perform a background check?

yes
Jon

what do they look for?

Anything that includes a felony
Jon

Look, I might have thrown some bottles, but it wasn't me who
urinated in that pool. Do you think these would get reported?

Evaluation

Location

Sometimes a recruiter may suggest an opportunity 3000 miles from your home in which you will have to work all week on site. To the untrained person, it may seem undesirable or even impossible to simply up and leave your family, friends and house for a job that might not work out.

Calm down, take a breath, and do not let this discourage you. A skilled recruiter will understand the unique challenges of your life (marriage, children, mortgage, etc.) better than yourself. They would never convince you to take that less-than-perfect opportunity for their personal gain.

NEW JOB OPENING, APPLY NOW!

DEAR ANTHONY,
We've identified you as a highly skilled candidate and we think your qualifications may be a great match for our newest open position. Please review the position details and contact us immediately if you are interested in being submitted.
Immediate Opening
[job details]
Sincerely,
Terry -----
Sr Technical Recruiter
----- INTERNATIONAL, INC.
BELLEVUE, WA 98004
(425) --- ---- | (877) --- ----

I am interested - what do you need from me?
Anthony

I need a current resume, work authorization status(country of citizenship), availability after offer acceptance.
Terry

what are their business hours?

Looks like this would be 7 to 3:30pm

That's fantastic. Would I get enough time to go home for lunch?

Scheduling would be coordinated w/ the manager

*In your opinion, Terry, do you think it would be simply
acceptable for me to go home during the day for lunch.*

Possibly, a matter to explore once you've started or at least if
you were to receive an interview request.

*The only reason I ask is because I live approximately 2,940 miles
away.*

Looks like you'd have to bring your lunch to work :)

*:) hope you have a good sense of humor. Enjoy your weekend
and Thanksgiving.*
Anthony

Subject:	Opening for Java Developer (Server Side) at Westbrook, ME
Sender:	Raj
Date:	22.02.2012
Background:	Northbrook, Eastbrook, Southbrook, Westbrook

Greetings,

My name is Raj and I'm an IT recruiter at ------Tech Solution. My number is (732) --------. Our records show that you are an experienced IT professional with experience in Java Development. This experience is relevant to one of my current openings.
[job details]
Sincerely yours,
Raj Roy

Thanks Raj.
How far is this from Eastbrook?

Hi, Thanks for your interest Eastbrook is in which state? please let me know....I can check

Which state is Westbrook in?

ME (Maine)

My apologies Raj - I meant to ask how far this is from Northbrook.

Would you like to know the distance from Northbrook or Eastbrook ?

Preferably Eastbrook. I just thought it would be easier for you to calculate from Northbrook, since it is just north of Southbrook.

In which state Eastbrook lies ?

I thought it was east of Westbrook??

Hi, I will check.
If you are interested, please send me your updated word format resume asap. If needed call back me at (732) --------
Regards
Raj

Raj,
I didn't hear back from you so I did some research.
It appears this is near Saddlebrook - is this right?

Answer: Westbrook is near by Portland, Falmouth of Maine (ME) State of USA ((Maine (ME) is situated at the top of right coast of USA))Please let me know your current location with the name of the State of USA If you are interested, please send me your resume....Thank you...
Regards
Raj

Thank you Raj.
Now what is Java?

Subject:	Java Developer Opportunities -3 years
Sender:	John
Date:	14.02.2012
Background:	Location, location, location.

Java Developer (3 positions), Contract Length: 3 years
Requested Start Date: ASAP, Tallahassee, Advanced Level
[job details]
John -----
----- Information Services, Inc.
Tallahassee, Florida 32303
(609) --- ----

John,
How far is this from Orlando?
Thanks,
Anthony

It will take 4 hours drive time in good traffic from Orlando,
florida to Tallahassee, Florida
John ------

Appreciate it John. Now how far is it from Long Island, NY,
where I live?

90

Subject:	java Architect-fulltime
Sender:	Geeta
Date:	02.02.2012
Background:	How close to the bell?

HI Anthony
In reference to your resume in our database, can you kindly look into the details and let me know your interest:
Position Type: Direct Hire
Location - City: Philadelphia, State: PA
[job details]
Thanks,
Geeta -----
-----, Inc
Woodbridge, NJ 07095
Ph: (732) --- ----

Is this near the Liberty Bell?

Probably YES.
THis is a Fulltime with INFOSYS technologies and the client is ----
---.
One of their offices is near to liberty bell, the rest i am not sure
Would you be interested?
Thanks,

I need to know how close to the freakin bell !!!
Thank you,
Anthony

around 10min
Thanks,

is that walking or by car?

Subject:	Server-Side Developer opportunity in San Francisco.
Sender:	Zack
Date:	09.12.2011
Background:	"Clang, clang, clang" went the trolley.

Hi Anthony,
You and I haven't spoken before but your name came up in a search for my client in San Francisco. They are a leader in mobile protection services. Based on your background in iOS Development and experience with Java/J2EE, I'd like to get in touch with you. Are you in the market for new positions? I hope to hear from you! If you are happily employed I'd love to be a resource for any of your friends or colleagues who may be looking.
Thanks!
Zack -----
Recruiter
----- Technology Partners
San Francisco, CA 94104
Direct: (415) --- ----
Cell: (925) --- ----

[job details]

Zack,
Do you think it would be possible for me to take the trolley to your client's site?
Thanks,
Anthony

Hi Anthony...So I need to explain a few things. The company currently has a branch in San Mateo. They are planning on moving that office to San Francisco by March of 2012. They are currently looking at commercial real estate in the financial district, but as of right now I don't know what building they are

planning on moving into. Let me know if I can answer any other questions.
Best,
Zack

Wow, I just wanted to know if there was a trolley that went from New York (where I live) to California, but thanks, lol !!!

Hi KkArora

Hope you are doing great! Please find the requirement below , If you find yourself comfortable with the requirement please reply back with your updated resume and I will get back to you or I could really appreciate if you can give me a call back at my contact number

[job details]

Thanks & Regards,

Mudit -----

Deputy Resource Manager

Consulting Redefined

----- Infotech, Inc.

Fremont, CA 94538

Phone : (408) --- ----

Mudit,

I find myself comfortable with the requirement.

But I am also wearing loose-fitting clothing and loafers

Do you have a copy of my resume?

Thanks,

Anthony

Hi Anthony,

I am not having your resume. Please provide me that and let me know that what rate you looking for on 1099 or C2C basis?

Regards,

Mudit

{attached fake resume}

Hi Anthony,
Resume is perfect let me know you easily relocate for this
position and let me know the rate on 1099 or C2C basis?
Regards,
Mudit

*when you refer to 'relocate' do you mean from like the kitchen
to the den, etc? that is quite easily done in my loose-fitting
clothes (pajamas right now).please advise.*

Working Conditions

A recruiter's insight can make all the difference in the world. All recruiters continuously visit each of their clients in an effort to remain 'in the know' with regard to the people and technologies they represent. They have to keep their 'finger on the pulse' of each organization and any changes that have recently occurred. Too bad, they are just a bunch of 'ass-wipes'.

Hi
I came across your resume from a portal and we have Sr Java
Developer in Milwaukee, WI location, Please advice if you would
be interested for this role, DETAILS L: ON W-2 ONLY
Location: Milwaukee, WI Hours per Day 8, Hours per Week 40
[job details]
Thanks!
Victor -----
IT Recruiter
----- International, Inc.
Phone: (888) --- ----
Desk: (636) --- ----

Victor, how many hours per week is this?

Anthony, Its Hours per Day 8,Hours per Week 40
Thanks!
Victor

*Would it be possible for me to work 10 hours per day on
Monday, Wednesday, Thursday and Friday for a total of 40
hours per week?*

I appreciate if you send me your resume I will check with my
Manager and do advice what's the hourly Pay rate you looking
for this position.
Thanks!
Victor

40 hours per week is fine, it's just that I am taking tuba lessons on Tuesday and am somehow looking to incorporate that into my weekly schedule. Do you understand?

You want to Take Tuesday off right, Well I can have my manager to Check with client end, Please advice
Thanks!
Victor

That would be optimum, but I am flexible if the client doesn't mind me bringing my tuba to the office each Tuesday.

You working throughout NY, You comfortable to relocate WI
Thanks!
Victor

My physical location can be anywhere ever since I found the tuba. My life was in a tailspin about a year ago - no money, no job, no throw pillows. It was only until I instituted 'Tuba Tuesdays' when my life (and spirit) became tuned to the peace of which the tuba brings. I don't expect you to understand the significance the tuba is to me, suffice to say that that the harmonious melodies it creates transcends my physical entity, thus my physical location. So, yea, I can relocate.

I just checked and Well I am afraid, Tuba lessons Will not go with client bummer :(
Thanks!
Victor

How about the harmonica?

Subject:	Need Java/j2ee developer with WSF experience - Des Moines, IA
Sender:	Bhushan
Date:	14.02.2012
Background:	Putting yourself in the best possible light..

Good Morning Sir.
You had applied to similar opening I had posted on dice.com on a previous occasion. Please apply to the below job freshly if you have experience with WSF (Web services Framework).I found your resume on my database. I felt you may have suitable skills for this requirement. Please review the Job description and let me know your interest. Please confirm your billing rate. Also confirm your availability so I can set up an interview for you ASAP. Please send me the following details as well.
[job details]
Thanks 'n' Regards
Bhushan -----
----- Inc.
P: (310) --- ----

Bhushan,
Thank you for the consideration - you are the man!!
I am available immediately - please let me know the next steps.
Thanks,
Anthony

I have already listed out what I need. Resume, contact info, visa status, availability and billing rate confirmation Please rush me the details and I will talk and submit the resume to the client.
Thanks 'n' Regards
Bhushan

Thank you very much Bhushan!

100

My resume is attached. Do you know if their office uses
fluorescent lighting? I much rather incandescent - those other
ones are fake shit, maybe good for plants. Please let me know.
Thanks,
Anthony

{attached fake resume}

I am unable to open resume due to some of the content.
Please send me a file with .doc extension instead of .docx. this
may solve the problem.
Thanks 'n' Regards
Bhushan

Bushan,
I have created a pdf for you - this is probably better.
What about the goddamn lights?
Thanks,
Anthony

{I didn't attach anything}

No attachment sir.
Yes! I found out. They do use fluorescent lights.
Thanks 'n' Regards
Bhushan

Sorry Bhushan, I must have hit send too fast. I have attached the
converted pdf file this time. Sounds like another place where I
have to bring in my own fuckin lamp.
Thanks,
Anthony

{attached second fake resume}

Size of Organization

There are fortune 100 corporations, which employ tens of thousands of people, and there are startups with only a handful at the helm. Based upon your personal criteria, the recruiter will help you determine the size of the organization in which you will be able to contribute and excel. Keep in mind - if you are not happy, the recruiter is not happy.

Dear Consultant,

We are looking for Java Developer for our client in Chicago, IL. Below are few details on it. Let me know if you would be interested / available for same. Please feel free to call / mail should you have any questions. Thanks!

[job details]

With regards,

Sam -----

Technical Recruiter

----- Group

Phone (630) --- ----

Downersgrove, IL, 6051

Is the client a little firm?

The below position is not for little firm. Thanks!

With Regards

Sam

Sam,

What about yourself -are you a little firm?

Thanks.

Subject:	Immediate Interviews- job opportunity :Websphere Administrator here in Dublin, Ohio.
Sender:	Marco
Date:	28.11.2011
Background:	Sometimes you have to be a little firm.

Hello,
We have a job opportunity:Websphere Administrator which we are trying to fill with here in Dublin, Ohio. please forward your consultants resume along with all the detail at the end of the email. Websphere Administrator Location: Dublin, Ohio Contract Length: 6months + - definite extension Interview Process: Phone to hire
[job details]
Thanks,
Marco -----
----- Global Inc.
Irving, TX 75038
Phone: (972) --- ----

Marco,
Thank you for the consideration.
Is your client a large firm?
Thanks,
Anthony

Yes. Its a large healthcare client and I am working with prime vendor.
Thanks & Regards
Marco

Marco,
Ok, that's good news.
I had another recruiter solicit me today and told me his client was a little firm (I thought this was a bit rude). Anyway, do you have any paperwork or forms I need to complete?

Thanks,
Anthony

Can you please forward your consultant's profile with expected rate per hour.
Thanks & Regards
Marco

Got it Marco, thanks.
I too am a little firm. Might be our conversation.
Anyway, I am open to market rate and dirty talk.
What else do you need?
Thanks,
Anthony

Benefits and Expenses

In addition to straight salary, benefits and expenses can help you reach your financial goals. You might be surprised what companies offer these days with regard to expenses.

Don't hesitate to ask your knowledgeable recruiter about the various benefits and expenses their client might offer.

Anthony Hello. My client is seeking a consultant for a six month contract. The position is based in Boca Raton, FL, however the first week will be spent in Tennesee. Client will pay travel. Would you be interested in learning more details?
[job details]
Thanks,
Charlie -----
Founder/CEO
T: (954) --- ----
C: (954) --- ----

Thanks Charlie.
What kind of working conditions do they offer?

They have a large office here in South Florida where you would work out of. Initially you would be in Tennessee. We would build the rate to include a per diem for a local hotel/transportation. I've been working with this client for about two years, and they are a very reputable company. I've had the opportunity to place several full time employees there. Charlie

Fair enough. Do they offer educational assistance?

This is a six month contract role so there is no tuition assistance.

That's too bad - I have almost completed a series of aviation courses to obtain my pilot's license. Would you please check for me? I feel this should be acceptable as it is relevant.

Yeah normally tuition reimbursement is paid out on courses that will have a direct impact on your performance at work, and_ _I don't see the connection with aviation courses. Again, this is contract and tuition expenses are only paid out to full time permanent employees. Sorry, I assume that this will not be the right fit for you. Thanks for your time.
  Charlie

I respectfully disagree Charlie.
If I do not obtain my pilot's license and purchase a small aircraft
for commuting, how would I make it to work on time,
considering this position is approximately 1,285 miles from my
house.
:)

Funny. Nice set up and delivery :)
If you are interested in the six month contract in SUNNY South Florida, we can talk shop.
Charlie

Charlie,
I'm glad you have a sense of humor.
Thanks again, and have a great Thanksgiving!
Anthony

Subject:	Brent from ---- - JAVA roles - WI or KY
Sender:	Brent
Date:	09.02.2012
Background:	Will they cover expenses?

Anthony,

Give me a call as soon as you get a chance. Here are the details for the two positions I have open that you would be great for. Just curious, what kind of rates do you typically bill for?
Location: Milwaukee, WI Duration: until 8/11/12Client: Energy Contract.
[job details]
Regards,
Brent L.
----- Associates, Inc.
(908) --- ----

Brent,
I typically bill $130/hr corp-to-corp plus expenses (massage, handjob, etc). Let me know your thoughts.
Thanks,
Anthony

Anthony,

Haha I don't know if I can take care of that last part for you. Let me ask the client and see what I can do haha. My thoughts are that neither role is going to be able to support the rates you deserve.

Just needed a smile before I went home.
You are a good sport.
I'm a JEE Architect in NY.
Have a good night.

110

Perks

Many organizations offer so many different perks to their employees; it can feel like wandering through a jungle without a machete. This is one area where the recruiter really shines. Through building meaningful relationships with the client and all personnel, the recruiter becomes privy to anomalies such as perks that would otherwise not be discussed nor offered. The recruiter wants to provide you with complete knowledge of these perks before you begin working for their client, so they can go to bat for you, trying to get everything you desire.

Subject:	Urgent need for a Java Developer........NJ and GA........Up to 30 month contract.......Potential right to hire.......No telecommute or remote.......See primary requirements below.
Sender:	Daniel
Date:	13.02.2012
Background:	What kind of perks do they offer?

My name is Daniel ------- and I'm a Recruiter at --------- LLC. You've received this email because the skills in your resume matched our search criteria for a Java J2EE Spring Developer in our database. It is possible that you may not be best suited for this particular position, but we have multiple positions available in all areas and levels of IT where you may be interested and better suited. Thank You and have a nice day!
[job details]
Sincerely Yours,
Daniel -----
(732) --- ----
----- LLC
Red Bank, NJ 07701

Thanks Daniel.
What start date are they looking for?

They will hire as soon as they find the right person. Typically 2-3 weeks from the date of the job offer.
Daniel

That sounds reasonable Daniel. Do you know of any outstanding 'perks' that your client might offer?

This is a contract Job. So no perks attached. However the position does hold the potential for full time hire with our client. At that point the package they can offer is quite substantial

Daniel

I've often heard that companies provide 'company car service' for employees that work rather late. The service would pick them up at the office and drive the employee directly to their house. Do you think your client might provide such a service?

No. not even a chance

what about blowjobs?

Subject:	Need Java Architect asap. Full time @ Naugatuck, CT.
Sender:	Venkat
Date:	01.12.2011
Background:	It's all about the coffee.

Hello ,
Please view the below Job Description and kindly do forward
the resume ASAP.
[job details]
Regards,
Venkat
Phone: (770) --- ----
----- Technologies Inc.

Yo Venkat. what's the salary?

Annual Salary:120k per annum
Regards,
Venkat

what about bonus, insurance, free coffee...

Please give me your contact no. I would like to discuss more abt
this
Regards,
Venkat

Venkat,
My resume is attached.
What is abt, and what type of coffee do they have?
Thanks,
Anthony

{attached fake resume}

Antony,
I am not clear please brief me the below. what type of coffee do they have? Please let me know your interest to this position if so I will go ahead and submit to this position and this position needs a face to face interview. Are you comfortable with it?
Regards,
Venkat

Venkat,
No worries - I wanted to know if they had Columbian, Kona, etc. There are other things that are more important. Do you drink coffee?
Thanks,
Anthony

Hi,

This is regarding a permanent job for Java J2EE in NYC, NY and Plano, TX, with ------- Technologies. Given below are the skills required for the job: Anticipating your quick response.

[job details]

Regards

Kumar -----

----- Inc

Woodbridge, NJ 07095

Direct : (732) --- ----

Which location is it???

Hi,

This is based out of New York City and Plano, TX. Please call for more details or give me a good time to call you.

Regards,

Kumar

I don't understand. Do I have to fly back and forth each day?

Hi,

These are 2 locations. You can join the one that suits you.

Regards,

Hold on, they are going to just GIVE me a suit?

Subject:	BI - Systems Analyst / Technical Project Manager positions in Redmond WA
Sender:	Indraraj
Date:	25.01.2012
Background:	Can I go home for lunch?

Dear Anthony

Our records show that you are an experienced IT professional with experience relevant to one of our current open position. Please let us know whether you would wish to evaluate one of the open positions we have with our customer based out of Redmond, VA. My firm -------- Technologies Inc. is headquartered in California and provides nationwide staffing support to our client.

[job details]

Regards,

Indraraj -----

Direct: (408) --- ----

Mobile: (240) --- ----

Milpitas, CA 95035

what would be the best commute for me?

Onsite

I meant what roads to take.

Camo,

Client is ----- who is the implementation partner and End client Is ---------.---------'WA office address is - "------- Redmond, WA 98052, United States".

Best Regards,

Indraraj

Indi,

would it be possible to go home for lunch?

Camo,
I can't commit anything behalf of my client. It totally depend on the company's policy.
Best Regards,
Indraraj

Fair enough, but in your professional opinion, if I establish a good working relationship with my manager, perform quality work on time, and ask for no other concessions, do you think it would be reasonable for me to go home for lunch?

Camo,
I think so. Its depend on your performance and your relationship with your reporting manager.
Best Regards,
Indraraj

Thank you Indi.
How long of a lunch would I get?

Camo,
Duration; 12 month initially and project is expendable.
Best Regards,
Indraraj

Indi,
I would like to know how long I have for lunch each day?

Camo,
Sorry I don't know. As per you experience you can guess what is working hours and what is lunch hour.
Best Regards,
Indraraj

That is what I was afraid of.

Camo,
You can discussed with project manager and still I am saying that I can't commit anything behalf of my client.
Best Regards,
Indraraj

I'm simply trying to gauge whether or not it is viable for me to go home for lunch.

Camo,
Now it up to you..if you like work with client then please share the profile or you can pass this position. Please let me know your decision.
Best Regards,
Indraraj

Well, since I live about 3000 miles away, I think I'll pass, lol.
:)

Camo,
Oops..but thanks to waste my time.. still Good luck for you career. :)
Best Regards,
Indraraj

Finalization

Negotiate Like a Champ

Every day each of us negotiates, whether it's scheduling a time to speak, or even allowing another vehicle to pass you on the highway. Why should negotiating with a recruiter be any different? Recruiters both anticipate and welcome all challenges to their initial offering. They realize the importance of your job to you and your family and are willing to put your financial needs ahead of their own.

Subject:	Java Developer/Lead/ San Fancisco, CA/ 12 to 18 Months
Sender:	Amit
Date:	13.02.2012
Background:	I explain why I'm the best candidate.

Greetings!!
I got your resume in our database and I think you might be a good match for the the position open with us, If you are qualified, available, interested, planning to make a change, or know of a friend who might have the required qualifications and interest, please respond with your updated resume and the following details:
[job details]
Thanks & Regards
Amit -----
Accounts Manager
----- Business Solutions
 P (732) --- ----

This sounds exciting Amit. How long have you been recruiting for this position?

This position opened on Friday and there are in total 7 spots to fill.

Amit,
I have 9 close friends that need jobs in addition to myself. How should I decide who gets a spot and who doesn't? Note: one guy has been a real dick lately and slept with another guy's wife.
Let me know.
Thanks,
Anthony

Anthony,

You can refer all 9 of your friends and your profile, I will submit all the profiles and rest depens on the "who has better knowledge and skills" criteria...
Regards
Amit

Whoa, slow down Amit. I emailed you first - why should any of those assholes get a crack at one of the openings before me. I say get me in, then these assholes, no. Let me know your thoughts.
Thanks.
Anthony,

Now you were the one who started the details about your friends, if you are interested in this position send me your updated resume along with the following details;
[details omitted]
Amit-----

I totally agree with you Amit. I should not have event mentioned those ball bags until after I secured one of the positions with you. You are right - fuck them. Anyway, my resume is attached. Please let me know the next steps.
Anthony

{attached fake resume}

Great resume,
Send me the following details as well:

[details omitted]

My answers are below. Just so you know, a few mins ago when I went to take a piss, I think one of those douche bags read my emails. If anyone should contact you saying I'm a reference, tell em to suck your dick and that they don't get shit until I'm all set, cool?

Subject:	Req: Strong java Developer with SQL skills - Mclean, VA
Sender:	Ram
Date:	15.02.2012
Background:	Don't sell yourself short.

Hi
One of our client in MCLEAN, VA is looking for a STRONG
JAVADEVELOPER WITH SQL SKILLS, If you have anyone please
send the resume with following Information.
[requested information]
Regards
Ram -----
----- Systems, Inc.
Princeton, NJ 08540
Phone: (609) --- ----

Ram,
My SQL is top-notch.
Please give your best rate.
Thanks,
Anthony

Rate $53/Hr on CtoC or 1099, Let me know
Thanks
Ram

Can you do 54/hour?

Yes, send me updated resume asap.
and what is your visa status?
Thanks
Ram

Ram,
My resume is attached.

126

Would 54.75/hr work?
Thank you,
Anthony

{attached fake resume}

Please resend me your resume...with .doc form
Thanks
Ram

Ram,
I opened the docx in Microsoft Word.
I then saved it as Word 97-2003 format.
The new file is attached here.
Is 54.50/hr acceptable?
Thanks,
Anthony

{attached second fake resume}

Still din't open..
Ram

Wow, I'm surprised.
Are you using a PC or a Mac?
I would like 55.25/hour now.
Thanks,
Anthony

Anthony,
I am having your old resume ... Do you want me to use?......I am
trying to reach you at 631.---.----.
Thanks
Ram

Ram,
How old is the resume?

Can I fax you my most current information.
I'd like 57.25/hour at this point.
What is your fax number?
Thanks,
Anthony

Why you are increasing rate?

My apologies Ram - I thought we were negotiating.
Is there a fax number to where I can send the updated
information?
Thanks,
Anthony

Anthony,
Please give me following info.
Full Name: Anthony------
Email id:a------@------------x.com
Contact No: 631.---.----
Current Location: work
Visa Status: citizen
Open to Relocate: no
Availability : immediate
Best Time to take call: any
Rate: 58.50/hr
Ram

I put the answers inline Ram.
Please let me know if there is any additional info you may need.
Thanks,
Anthony

631.---.---- not working..

Ram,
Something seems to be wrong with the phone line.

Can I fax the information and resume to you?
Rate is 59/hr. What is your fax number?
Thanks,
Anthony

Please send with word doc..

Ram,
Let's give this another shot.
I brought it into Word for the Mac.
Attached is the latest resume.
My rate is now 60.25 plus expenses.
Please let me know if this does not open.
Thanks,
Anthony

{attached third fake resume}

Tried many times...does not open..

Ram,
I don't know what to tell you - use a crowbar to open it???
Do you want me to mail or fax it to you? Unfortunately, my rate
will now be 62.50 plus expenses plus signon.
Get back to me asap!!!
Anthony

Subject:	JAVA developer reqd for my Direct client at MO---only US citizens please...........
Sender:	Surya
Date:	29.11.2011
Background:	No one gets hurt in a win-win.

HII..!!! PARTNERS,
HOPE YOU ARE DOING WELL.
I WOULD LIKE TO PRESENT YOU AN AWESOME JOB OPENING WITH ONE OF MYCLIENT. KINDLY FIND THE JOB DESCRIPTION GIVEN BELOW AND IF YOU HAVE ANY CONSULTANT AVAILABLE FOR THIS POSITION PLEASE REPLY ME BACK WITH HIS UPDATED RESUME ALONG WITH HIS CONTACT DETAILS.YOUR QUICK RESPONSE WILL BE HIGHLY APPRECIATED......!!!!! PLEASE DON'T SUBMIT CANDIDATES WITHOUT MATCHING WITH JOB DETAILS.
[job details]
Thanks
Surya -----
(248) --- ----
----- Systems Inc

Hi ,
Please send me your resume. This is for the client ---------------.
We wont be having a margin ...Please agree to take up the project at40$/hr on w2.... i can for 40.5$/hr on w2..

40.72 and it's a deal.

Hi,
I have agreed to the rate of 41$/hr on w2..please rush me your resume and send me details... I have very less time for submission.. Please...
Thanks & Regards,
SURYA

Surya,

Can you do 41/hr?

Hi,
I just talked to my manager, and they told me to proceed ahead with 41$/hr on w2 for the right consultant. So Please send me your resume and details so that I can submit you to the client right away..
Thanks & Regards,
SURYA

I meant $42 Surya, sorry.

HI,
I think you are playing...sorry...even if you send your resume.. I wont submit.....
Thanks & Regards,
SURYA

You are a fine negotiator Surya. I will accept the $41/hour. Please submit me and let me know the feedback as soon as possible.
Anthony

Hi ,
Sorry I didn't mean to hurt you in any way. Where is your resume for me to submit...Please also send me the details I asked......Only of this req I have asked for that rate for any other req I will give you the best....Please send me your current resume along with the following information:
1. Full Name:
2. Current Location:
3. Phone #:
HOME/CELL/WORK
4. Email:
5. Rate: $ W-2 / All Inclusive on 1099 /corp. to corp
6. Work Status (Citizen/Green Card/EAD/H-1):
7. Availability (How soon can your join):

8. Please attach your current resume.
9.Last 4 digits of your SSN:
Thanks & Regards,
SURYA

well it did hurt a bit Surya (mostly in the balls). here is the info:

{provided fake info}

Hi Anthony,
You didn't attach any resume.. please send me resume.....
Thanks & Regards,
SURYA

apologies - it is here now. my balls hurt so much I had to ice-water-teabag them. please confirm upon receipt.
thanks.

{attached fake resume}

Subject:	Requirement : Java with spring and hibernate : Foster City, CA
Sender:	Hemant
Date:	21.02.2012
Background:	Understand the terms.

Hi,

I have some urgent requirements with my direct client – Toyota Financial Services. Please send me your updated resume, if interested.

[job details]

Warm Regards,

Hemant -----

----- Inc

San Jose, CA 95113

Phone: (408) --- ----

Desk: (408) --- ----

Hemant,
I am very interested.
What are the lease terms?
Thank you,
Anthony

Hi Anthony,

I have this position with --------- and they are looking for a local resource who has financial experience too. This is a contract position and the rate is $50-52 per hour all inclusive on 1099. Let me know if this works with you.

Thanks & Regards,

Hemant

Hemant, I thought this was with Toyota.

Hi Alexander,

This position is with --------- and not with Toyota. let me know if you are interested to work with ---------
Thanks & Regards,
Hemant

I understand. What type of cars does --------- make?

Where does the car came from? --------- do not make any cars. They are supporting the end customer for this role who is a financial client.
Thanks & Regards,
Hemant

I need to know in order to compare leasing terms.
ie, compact, midsize, sedan, etc.
Do you understand?

Hi Alex,
It is a midsize car.
The hourly rates are $55 per hour all inclusive at 1099 / C2C.
Let me know your thoughts.
Thanks & Regards,
Hemant Kothari

I was more interested in a sedan, say around $60/hour.

Sorry, Alex.
$55 is the best. let me know if it works with you.
Thanks & Regards,
Hemant

Hemant,
I suppose that would work.
Is there any money down or balloon payment at the end?
Also, what transportation fees and taxes?
Thank you,
Anthony

Hi Alex,
Can you tell me your current location as I am looking for local resources.
Thanks & Regards,
Hemant

{I did not reply}

Subject:	Iphone Application developer – IL
Sender:	Sandeep
Date:	22.11.2011
Background:	Bean counter.

Hello Anthony,
Greetings!!! Hope you are doing well !!!
Please go through the below requirement and revert to
sandeep@-----associates.com with updated resume.
[job details]
Thanks & regards
Sandeep -----
----- Associates LLC
Hilliard, OH 43026
Work: (614) --- ----

Sandeep,
Thank you for the consideration.
Would you know the rate range?
Thanks.

Hello Anthony,
Greetings!!!
Thanks for your response, please quote the best rate.
Thanks & regards
Sandeep

I'm sorry Sandeep, I don't understand 'quote the best rate'.
Does this mean I should guess the highest hourly rate that
others have submitted to you? If so, this is similar to guessing
the most jellybeans in the jar at Easter. I was never very good at
this.

Hello Anthony,
I would appreciate if you could provide me the contact number
or you can give a call to my phone number please.

Thanks & regards
Sandeep

I am currently at work and need to be discreet. You didn't answer my jellybean question.

Hello Anthony,
I Can go for $60 - $65/hr on 1099, please let me know.
Thanks & regards
Sandeep

Thank you Sandeep, but please, please, answer my friggin' jellybean question!

Subject:	JAVA Fulltime/Contract positions with --- North America.
Sender:	Arvind
Date:	08.12.2011
Background:	Arvind has a bit of a spelling problem, but I try to make him as comfortable as possible during *"regural business business hours"*.

GREETINGS!
We are currently recruiting for --- with revenues of ~$99 Billion and a Global work force of 425,000. --- is in the midst of nationwide Java/J2ee/SOA rollouts and is seeking qualified JAVA talent in various Java Technologies
[job details]
Arvind -----
----- Solutions
Direct: (703) --- ----

what is the location?

Hi Anthony,
Right now I have a position in Waltham, MA and the best rate is $55/hr on w2.if this works for you send me your word doc resume ASAP its real urjent.
Arvind

I agree - urjency matters, but first a few questions:
1. What are the business hours?
2. What is the dress code?
3. Would you be able to pay $60/hr corp-to-corp?
Thanks,
Anthony

Hi Antony,

First thing is corp-to-corp doesn't work out and coming to dress code its as usual formal dress in regural business business hours.
Arvind

Ok Arvind, just 2 more:
1. regural business business hours is fine
2. W2 is fine, but can you do a bit higher?
Thank you,
Anthony

Hi Antony,
$50/hr on w2 and company will pay the tax you don't need to pay your taxes. I have a couple of questions regarding your experience?
1. how many years of experience do you have with java, j2ee, spring, hibernate and struts?
2. what is your visa status?
3. in the recent past have you ever been presented to ---?

Arvind,
one more quick question:
1. how can I be w2 if the company pays my taxes?
Thanks,
Anthony

Hi Antony,
We will be paying your regular taxes and in hand you would be getting $55/hr and this is the best rate from ---. if you are interested send me your word doc resume and call me ASAP because we can't close the deal without talking.
Arvind

Arvind,
one more quick question:
1. is there a possibility to work remotely?

Thank you,
Anthony

No
Thank you so much.
Arvind

I understand Arvind, and appreciate your quick replies. Now, considering that your client's location is approximately 225 miles from my home, I have one more question:
1. would you be able to ask your client to either cancel their current building lease or sell their building, purchase or lease one a bit closer to me, and notify all of their employees that they are relocating to accommodate my commute? If so, I might have some more questions for you to answer, lol.
Thank you,
Anthony

Resigning Tactfully

You many think that a recruiter's job is complete once finding and helping you get an offer from another company, but did you know that as a professional courtesy, they will provide you tactful approaches for you to take when resigning from your current job? Further providing the recruiter with a sense of accomplishment and fulfillment, assisting you with your exit strategy is among their core competencies.

Hi Anthony, Hope you are doing well! I'm Gayathri from ---------
IT Solutions! I have the below opportunity with our direct client.
Please send me your resume if you are interested. Feel free to
call or email me if you have any questions. I look forward to
speaking with you.
[job details]
Gayathri M
----- IT Solutions
Farmington Hills, Michigan 48334
Ph : (301) --- ----

Yee-hah. Thank you for the consideration.
Is this spot available immediately?

Yes it is.
This is an immediate position. The maximum notice period to
join is 2 weeks. This is a long term opportunity.
Gayathri M

I'm not sure I understand.
Who would I send notice to?

Hi Anthony,
I meant, interviews will happen immediately but the max time
client can wait for you to join is 2 weeks.
Gayathri M

Thank you Gayathri. I think I understand.

142

I thought I would have to notify my current boss, but from what you are telling me, it seems that I don't have to tell him anything - just stop showing up once I get this new job.

Sorry if I confused you. Looks I'm not communicating right. Once you finish the interview and the new cleint selects you, normally you need to inform your current boss and will give them 1 or 2 week notice to relieve you from the project. After you get releived, you will join the new client. In short we call it as 2 week notice.
Gayathri M

Now I get you, but if I tell this guy, he's gonna be very mad. Can you tell him?

Subject:	Urgent requirement for Application/SW Development @ MORRISVILLE, NC
Sender:	Aftab
Date:	28.11.2011
Background:	Tough working environment.

Hi ,

My name is Aftab with --- Technologies Inc. Please go through the below requirement and let me know your interest ASAP . Reply with your update resume, visa status, notice period and expected hourly rate.

[job details]

Thanks and regards

Aftab -----

----- Technologies Inc.

Phone: (404) --- ----

Alpharetta, GA 30022

Aftab,

Thank you so much for the consideration.

I believe I am qualified (possibly overqualified).

What would you like me to do next?

Hi,

Thanks for responding, Please reply with your update resume, visa status, notice period and expected hourly rate.

Best Regards

Aftab

What is a notice period?

How soon you can join once you been offered for this position. Is it Immediate, one week, 2 week etc.

I can start one week from today, big man!

Sounds good, I appreciate if you send me your updated resume and best number to reach you.
Best regards

My resume is attached.
Can't talk at work - my boss will have a fit. He actually threw a stapler at this guy for calling his wife (seriously). Tough environment, that's why I'm looking to get out.
Thanks.

{attached fake resume}

Hello Anthony,
Thanks for sending your resume, I really appreciate your time and patience on this regard. I tried reaching you over phone on 631---------, and left a voice mail too, but no luck. I would like to represent your profile for this position. Let me give you a quick note on this position. This position is with my end client ----, initially it's a 12 months contract and might be extend up to 3 years. Max pay rate on W2 is $65/H without benefits. There is an ---- system called x-----, all contract position are represented from this system to the client ----. For submission purpose we require your First and Last legal name which appears on your Social card and whole 9 digit SSN. Please find the ---- submission SCREEN SHOT DETAILS BELOW, The system needs your complete 9 digits SSN# to submit your profile and proceed with the interview process. Looking forward for your response at the earliest so that we could speed up the recruitment process.
Best Regards
Aftab

Aftab,
I actually need more than patience at this place - it requires rabbit-like reflexes to avoid all the crap this guy throws at you. Seriously, I can't understand how throwing fruit and office supplies at your subordinates can be a long-term motivational technique. Rumor has it that he also exposed himself to Sophie,

but she didn't have her camera phone with her. Anyway, the rate is fine, so please submit me at your convenience.
Thanks,
Anthony

Okay, I will submit but for submission purpose I require your First and Last legal name which appears on your Social card and whole 9digit. Is it possible to send those details in an email? So that I go ahead and submit your profile and complete this submission process.
Regard
Aftab

I just got hit with a friggin banana. My full name is Anthony Alcamo. The last 4 of my SSN is 4286. This place is starting to smell like a fruit salad.

Thanks Anthony, But to upload your resume, in the ---- system which is called x-----, I require whole 9 Digit SSN.
Regards
Aftab

Aftab,
Ok, but please do not share with anyone other than the client: 644-91-4286. On another note, this maniac now has nothing but boots on with a nerf blaster full of raw eggs, flapping his arms like a chicken screaming 'THIS IS EGGS-HILARATING'! Have you ever heard of someone doing something so ridiculous? I'm just afraid to call anyone for help cause I really need this job. Will you let me know once I have been submitted?
Thanks,
Anthony

Thanks for the Info, however as mention in the Job requirement please confirm that After Initial round of phone interview, you are will come for In person interview at the client site on your own cost.

Best Regards
Aftab

Aftab,
I confirm that after the phone interview I will make myself
available for an in-person interview. On another note, you will
not believe this- my boss is now balancing himself on the water
cooler, nothing on but boots, shooting glasses, and now he is
inserting red grapes up his butt and 'farting' them at my
coworkers. This is like a bad movie. I want to just take off my
3D glasses and leave the theater, but it's completely real and
very scary. Is there anything you could suggest I do until I get
this interview with your client?
Anthony

I will keep you posted once I hear from the client.
Take care, have a nice working day ahead.
Best Regards
Aftab

Oh crap, Aftab, he just brought out the pumpkins - I thought he
used 'em all up on Halloween, but now it looks like he's been
hittin' the pipe again, and there's pumpkin tendrils, pulp and
goop everywhere. I swear, I would never get high and hurl
pumpkin parts (even at my gay bang-swinger parties). Please
advise.

Good Fortune

Any candidate that follows all of the advanced techniques I've provided in this book can still benefit by some means of good fortune. In the page(s) that follow, I will briefly recall a touching story which conveys this true meaning.

Subject:	Job opening//Sr. Java/J2EE developer/Architect // Philadelphia, PA // 12 Months
Sender:	Sudha
Date:	08.12.2011
Background:	A 'Resouring Specialist' helps bring me good fortune.

Hello,

This is SUDHAMADHURI with SYSTEL INC, We have a requirement for the below position so please do reply with your updated resume if you are available for new projects ASAP. To know more about us, please visit www.---------.com.

[job details]

Thanks& Regards

Sudha -----

Resouring Specialist

------ Inc.

Atlanta, Georgia 30328

Direct: (678) --- ----

Phone: (678) --- ----

Sudha,

What a coincidence. I read my horoscope this morning and it said 'A stranger will bear a great surprise to you'. I suppose you are the stranger, and this opportunity is the surprise (not sure about the bear). Anyway, do you have a copy of my resume?

Thanks,

Anthony

Please send me your updated resume and also let me know the best rate you are looking for this position.

Thanks & Regards

Sudha

{attached fake resume}

Sudha,
My resume is attached. If you were to ask me this question last week, I would have said 'market rate', but this past Tuesday I had Chinese food, and in my fortune cookie, it said 'Don't settle - the world will bring you all that you desire', so I'm thinking that it's possible I could get a larger rate. What are your thoughts?
Thanks,
Anthony

Continuation

Continued Correspondence

Even after you land that perfect job, it is important to maintain close relationships with the most seasoned recruiters. One technique that I find useful is the auto-responder. This lets the recruiter know that you are currently employed or on assignment, but you'd like to remain in close contact with them in order to keep future mutually beneficial opportunities available.

Subject:	Get me off
Sender:	Nicole
Date:	21.02.2012
Background:	I send an email to Nicole making it appear as if it was sent via auto responder (automatic email reply).

Hi Anthony
Could you let me know if you are actively searching for a new position? We have the following opening currently available with our direct client. Please review quickly and let me know if you or a friend / colleague might be interested? If this is a role you are interested in, please send me a Word resume. I will need that to get in front of the recruiters for the position.
Project Manager - Mobile Applications, Location: San Jose, CA
[job details]
Best Regards,
Nicole -----
Solution Manager
We want to hear from you but please email me instead of calling me. I get hundreds of voicemails a day and simply cannot respond to them all! Thanks!
- Trust us to deliver!

Thank you for your email.
You have been added to our biweekly fundraiser distribution.
If this is in error, please reply with 'Get me off' in the subject.
Team AA

Get me off
Best Regards,
Nicole

Nicole,
I received your request, and sorry for any inconvenience.
Please confirm that you would like me to get you off.

156

Thanks,
Anthony

Confirmed.
Best Regards,
Nicole

Nicole,
Before I get you off, would you like to go for cocktails?
Thanks,
Anthony

HI,
My client is looking for JAVA J2EE ARCHITECT for FULL TIME
PERMANENT EMPLOYMENT in CUPERTINO CA.
[job details]
Thanks and regards,
Gulzar -----
Phone #: (480) --- ----
-------- LLC
Tempe AZ 85284

Thank you for your email.
You have been added to our biweekly fundraiser distribution. If
this is in error, please reply with 'Get me off' in the body of your
email.
Team AA

Get me off
Thanks and regards,

Gulzar,
That is inappropriate you pervert!

This is Michelle- part of Talent Acquisition. I wanted to take the opportunity to keep you aware that ------- Technologies is now open to Hire Immediate Hiring at and many more locations. Please do attach a copy of your recent updated resume.
[job details]
Michelle -----
----- Inc
Woodbridge, NJ 07095
Direct : (732) --- ----

We appreciate any contribution(s). You have been added to our biweekly fundraiser distribution. If this is in error, please reply with 'Get me off' in the body of your email.
Thank you,
Team AA

Get me off

Michelle,
I am in receipt of your emailed request.
Please confirm that you would like me to get you off.
Thanks,
Anthony

Yes

Michelle,
I am flattered. Perhaps we might go to dinner and a movie first?
Thanks,
Anthony

Keep Their Attention

Adding some flair to your emails will certainly get the recruiter's attention. You may be wondering, if shock therapy and hitting the recruiter with a big stick will also get their attention. The answer is yes, albeit in a more negative manner. In the examples that follow, we use a positive, motivational, and reinforcing tone.. This section will explore some rhyming techniques that will really pack a punch!

Subject:	Sr. Java/J2EE Developer -- Nashville TN -- Full Time
Sender:	Sri G.
Date:	02.12.2011
Background:	Complete the rest, then big sausage fest!

Dear Anthony,

Hope you are doing good...!!!

This is SRI ----- from ------ Consulting Group. I have a very urgent requirement with one of my DIRECT CLIENT. Please go through the requirement below and let me know if you are comfortable.

[job details]

Thanks

Sri -----

(502) --- ----

----- Consulting Group, Inc.

Louisville, KY 40223

Sri,

This looks exciting and I have the skills.

How long before the spot gets filled?

Thanks,

Anthony

Dear Anthony

Thanks for the immediate reply and interest in the position. I would appreciate if you can forward me your contact number so that I can have a small discussion with you on the requirement. This is a very urgent requirement which has to be filled within the coming week.

Thanks

Sri

I can't use the phone - boss is a deek.

Perhaps we can discuss next week?

Dear Anthony,
Thanks once again for the reply. To go ahead with the process of submitting your profile to the client, I require from you, the following details [details required are marked in red, please fill all the fields].
[details]

There's a lot of info required below.
I'll send it to you, but I type rather slow.
How soon do you need it? By the end of the day?
Might we hookup this weekend to discuss? are you gay?

Dear Anthony,
Please send me the details before end of the day today. Or if not possible, by Monday morning, as I will not be available at the workplace to submit your profile to the client.
Thanks
Sri

I'll try to have all of it done by tonight.
Per chance would you be interested in a sword fight.
By Monday I should be complete with the rest.
Then maybe we could go to a big sausage fest.
Please advise.

Hi,
This is Madhukar with ------- Technologies, Inc. We are looking
for a Java Architect for our client in Central IL. Please review the
following requirement and let me know your interest.
[job details]
Regards,
Madhukar
------- Tech
(678) --- ----

Thank you Madhukar! When I saw Illinois,
I thought..oh boy, oh golly, oh gee, oh boy!
My resume is here. This position looks great.
Let me know what you think, and what is the rate?

Dear Anthony,
Could you please send me you updated word document for
further process.
Thanks
Madhukar

That's fine Madhukar.
I attached it for you.
Please check it out, biatch.
Let me know what to do.

{attached fake resume}

Dear Anthony,

Thanks for sending your resume unfortunately the client is looking for Java Architect but not an oracle Database Administrator. I will keep you posted of oracle admin requirements if any of my clients have an opening.
Thanks
Madhukar

I am a Java Architect.
That's what I do.
Read the resume, biatch.
I sent it to you.

Hi

Hope you are doing great! Please find the requirement below, If you find yourself comfortable with the requirement please reply back with your updated resume and I will get back to you or I would really appreciate if you can give me a call back at my contact number 408--------- EXT:-329.LOCATION: New Albany, OH Duration: 3+ Months. Must be able to start from Monday! [job details]

Prateek -----

Technical Resource Specialist

----- Infotech, Inc.

Fremont, CA 94538

Phone : (408) --- ----

Prateek,
This position sounds good, and three months is a start.
My resume's attached. Did you just hear me fart?
Let me know if there's anything else that you need.
This is so funny, I think I just peed.
Anthony

{attached fake resume}

.Doc file not open
(Technical Resource Specialist)

I thought I provided that info before.
I live in New York, unlike you, you big wh0re.

166

Current location plz???
Thanks And Regards,
Prateek Jain

{attached second fake resume}

Yeah, that one was bad, try this one instead.
Please let me know what you think, and if you'll give me head.

HI,
MY NAME IS ANDREW ------ AND I'M A RECRUITER WITH ------- --- IN HARRISBURG, PA. I AM CONTACTING YOU BECAUSE YOUR RESUME IS ONDICE.COM AND IT CAME UP ON A SEARCH FOR A JAVA ARCHITECT OPENING WE HAVE WITH OUR CLIENT, ------------------, IN CAMP HILL, PA. THEPOSITION WOULD BE A 6 MONTH+ CONTRACT ON A W-2 BASIS.
[job details]
THANKS FOR LOOKING!
Andrew ------
Technical Recruiter
Harrisburg, PA 17111
Phone: (717) --- ----
Mobile: (717) --- ----

Andrew,
I see you work for -------- Aid.
This spot is a bit too far I'm afraid.
Working remotely would work for me.
Please go check with the client and see.
Anthony

Hi Anthony,
Thanks for touching base with me. They want someone who can work in Camp Hill.
Have a good weekend.
-Andrew

Camp Hill does sound nice.
Please see about 4 days per week.
Ten hours per day.

Then we can speak.

That might be a possibility. What are you looking for rate-wise if they're willing to do 4-tens? Also, would you mind sending me a Word copy of your resume?
Andrew

market rate will be fine. attached is my profile.
please let me know if this spot is worthwhile.

Andrew - I'm surprised he wasn't interested since our rate to him would have been $150/hr. - keep looking....

now Bill that's just hurtful, since all that I seek
is really high pay and a 4-day work week.
2-3 months vacation, a desk and a phone
checks directly deposited as I sometimes stay home.
calling in sick as a weekly occurrence
bad weather and traffic would be no deterrence.
but I'm sure even if I were a perfect match,
you'd probably take it yourself and tell me to scratch.
Have a great holiday,
Anthony

Subject:	Urgent direct client requirments still require consultants(Hyperion Administrator, Core Java Developer Financial, Oracle DBA with 11g)
Sender:	Parikshit
Date:	02.12.2011
Background:	Parikshit …. almost sounds like a bird turd.

HI,
WE AT ------ ARE STILL HIRING CONSULTANTS FOR
REQUIREMENTS MENTION BELOW.
Title: Hyperion Administrator
Duration: long term
Location: Hartford, CT or CO
[job details]
Thanks and Regards,
Parikshit -----
----- Technology Inc.
Iselin, New Jersey 08830
Work : (732) --- ----

Parikshit,
I am comfortable with the tools that they use
My resume's attached for you to peruse.
With regard to the req, it's perfect as such.
Is there anything else I may send to you, biatch?
Thank you,
Anthony

{I didn't attach anything}

Sir,
Thanks for reply. Resume was not attached with this mail.
Please attach the same and send me.
Parikshit

My mistake. Please try now.

170

I must have overlooked it somehow.
As far as the comp, please let me know.
I am comfortable with market rate, ho.

{attached fake resume}

Miscellaneous

Some emails will require more thought as to their classification, but certainly deserve the credit of being presented here. The insightful nuggets that follow are meant to possibly fill any gaps that may still exist. To paraphrase, I continue to break their balls.

Subject:	Excellent opportunity for Java tech lead with Capital One.
Sender:	Run Dil
Date:	21.02.2012
Background:	Run with it.

Hi,
Location: Waukesha, WI
Job Type : Fulltime
Total positions: 6
CORE JAVA DEVELOPERS- MEDICAL DOMAIN
[job details]
D. RUN -------
Phone : (973) --- ----

Run Dil,
Your name sounds familiar. Were you in the last NYC
Marathon? Anyway, I would like to be considered for this
position. What do I need to do next?
Thanks,
Igoes Fast

Send me your resume.

Why don't you just run over here and get it?

Hi,
My name is . I am an Executive in Intellectual Capital Development with -------- Inc. Our Team has been assisting Clients on their critical Projects. I came across your resume through www.-------.com. I would like to check your availability and Interest for this opportunity.
[job details]
Thanks & Regards,
Praveen -----
Executive - Intellectual Capital Development
----- Inc.
Middlesex, NJ 08846
Phone: (732) --- ----

Praveen,
Congratulations, when do I start?
Anthony

Hi Anthony
Please send me the resume to checked and get back to you
Thanks & Regards,
Praveen

It is attached in word doc format.
I feel like I hit the lottery!

{attached fake resume}

Hi anthony
Your Sending resume is not open due to some error can you please send me again

Thanks & Regards,
Praveen
Executive - Intellectual Capital Development

I just fell down the stairs.
What is the submission deadline?

Hi Anthony
The client is moving very fast so we want to submit asap
Thanks & Regards,
Praveen

Dude, moving too fast is what caused me to fall.
Do you know where the fibula bone is? I think I have a problem
with it now. Will they require any type of endurance tests? I
may have to wait until after the x-rays.
Please advise.
Anthony

Dear Anthony,

Hope you are doing great.

This is Irfan from V Soft. We are a staffing firm that deals with contract and full time placement. I am looking for a SR. JAVA DEVELOPER FOR 6 MONTHS CONTRACT AT LOUISVILLE, KY.

Please send me your updated resume in WORD format along with expected hourly rate & availability.

[job details]

Thanks & Regards,

Irfan -----

----- Consulting Group, Inc.

Louisville, KY 40223

(502) --- ----

Ifran,

What comes after 6 months?

Dear Aalcamo,

This project will end after 6 months.

Thanks & Regards,

Irfan

wrong, you silly, 7 months comes after 6 months - it's basic math. do you have a copy of my resume or do you need one?

Dear Aalcamo,

I don't have your resume, could you please send me your resume.

Thanks & Regards,

Irfan

Irfan,
One (1) copy of my resume is attached here.
If you previously did not have a copy, you had zero (0).
You should now have one (1) copy of my resume (i.e. 0+1=1).
Thank you,
Anthony

{attached fake resume}

Dear Anthony,
I am unable to open your resume, could you please resend in word for.doc format. The attached file has encountered some problem.
Thanks & Regards,
Irfan

{attached second fake resume}

I understand Irfan.
I am attaching one (1) more copy in pdf format.
Along with the zero (0) you had, and one (1) I sent previously,
you should now have a total of two (2) copies (0+1+1).
Thank you,
Anthony

{attached third fake resume}

Subject:	Permanent Opportunity
Sender:	Diem
Date:	29.11.2011
Background:	Location is important, so I gave him the coordinates of my dinghy.

Hi Anthony,
I left you a message today because I came across your profile and thought you'd be a good fit for an open position I have. Although is it in the Denver office, this position would sit in Montvale, NJ. Below my signature line is the job description. Is there a good time to call you to discuss this?
[job details]
Thanks,
Diem
Technical Recruiter
Greenwood Village, CO 80111
T: (303) --- ----

Let's go for it Diem.

Hi Anthony,
Is there a good time to call you to discuss the details of this opportunity?
Thanks,
Technical Recruiter

My boat won't dock until Friday. If you are in a hurry, I can ask the captain if he'll let me take the dinghy. Please advise.

No Worries Anthony we can wait until then.

Diem,
It's all good. The dinghy should be seaworthy for up to 12 miles (although I might be about 142 from shore). Captain said he'll even provide me with some communication equipment. I don't

know how safe this will be, but I'd really like a shot at this job. If you do not hear from me within 16 hours, my current coordinates are 28°29'20?N 80°34'40?W? / ?28.48889°N 80.57778°W.
Be well,
Anthony

Hi Anthony:
I am a recruiter with ------- Systems and during my search for
JAVA APPLICATIONS ENGINEER. I ran across your resume on one
of the job portals. Your resume seems to be a good fit for this
position so please see below the brief job description and let
me know your interest in it.
[job details]
Thanks and regards,
Raksha -----
Recruiter
----- Systems Inc.
(732) --- ----

Raksha,
My resume is attached.
thank you.

{I didn't attach anything}

Hi Anthony:
I couldn't find your resume attached, I guess you missed it.
Thanks and regards,
Raksha

My apologies Raksha, I'm using a different browser - please try
now.

{I still didn't attach anything}

Hi Anthony:

Good morning! But unfortunately I didn't see any attachment in this mail as well.
Thanks and regards,
Raksha

Raksha,
I think I might have a virus on my machine - every time I start up Safari, it navigates to chixwithdix.com and then many popups are loaded. I'm trying again with Opera - let me know if you get it this time.
Thanks,
Anthony

{this is complete bullshit, also check the website name}

All right Anthony...
I will let you know once I receive your resume.
Thanks and regards,
Raksha

Raksha,
I attached it to my last email - sorry if it did not get through - maybe this time. Those foul popups continue and my monitor looks like a complete sausage-fest. I had to turn the sound off. I would really like to get this process moving, however, so is there another way of getting my resume to you very quickly? Maybe FTP, courier, pony-express, or something?
Thanks,
Anthony

Hi Anthony:
Thank you for the patience.
Please try sending it to my colleague's id aj@-------sys.com . He is using safari so it might work there.
Thanks and regards,
Raksha

AJ,

Raksha suggested that I try to email my resume to you. My computer seems to be real frigged up at the moment. Most of my icons have been replaced with female body parts. When I open up my main browser, it displays images from a Turkish prison. Unreal. Anyway, please see if you can open the attached resume. If so, would you please forward to Raksha.
Thanks,
Anthony

{I didn't attach anything for AJ either. I'm surprised he has the same issue, lol}

There was no attachment with the email you sent. Can you copy paste your resume in response to this email. I hope it is not too much of a hassle considering the problems you are facing with your computer.
Regards,
AJ ------
Recruiter
------- Systems, Inc.
Work: 770---------

{I give them both an hour or two to compose themselves}

Hi Anthony:
I tried finding your resume on Monster and I found the one attached to this mail. Hope you can find this one attached. About the pay rate, this position is with Nike and they can offer around 75/hr on W 2. So please let me know your thoughts on this.
Thanks and regards,
Raksha

Raksha,
You can use this for now Raksha, but it doesn't include some of my most recent experience like Spring, Hibernate, Burlesque

*Dancing, etc. See if the client will accept this - if not I can take a
written test, dance for him/her, whatever. Is this acceptable?*
Thanks,
Anthony

Hi Anthony:
I can forward this one for the time being. Please let me know
the good time to talk to you regarding this position. Actually the
Java applications position is on hold as of now I just checked
and now I have another position, which is server side
Engineer/Java position. Its description is as follows:

[job description]

Please let me know your thoughts on this position.
Thanks and regards,
Raksha

Raksha,
*This one sounds even better. I pole dance also. Should I try to
send an updated resume geared for this particular spot. Maybe
a picture of me on the pole? Please let me know.*
Thanks,
Anthony

Anthony:
Could you please let me know your contact details to reach out
to you for this position, as I need to discuss this position before
moving ahead in the process.
Thanks and regards,
Raksha

Raksha,
*As far as contact details, Anthony is fine. In the past I would go
by Tony, but have since phased that out. You can also call me
dude, bro, cap'n, etc. I even have a old group of buddies that*

still call me Carpet-Bob (nuf said here). Whatever you think the
client will respond to is fine with me.
Thanks,
Anthony (Carpet-Bob)

Dear <CandidateNickname>
Zeeland, MI, Contract to Hire or Direct Hire
My client is looking for an Embedded SW Engineer with a very strong C backround. Also they must have at least 8 years of embedded experience. My client is willing to hire Direct or contract to hire. They are working on installing cameras in the rear-view mirrors of vehicles. Please get back to me and I will give you more info on the position.
[job details]
Jason -----
Account Coordinator
----- Express, Inc.
Technical Staffing
Wakefield, MA 01880
T: (781) --- ----

Thanks Jason. How well do you know the hiring manager?

We have a very good relationship with hiring manager.
Are you interested?
Jason

Yes. Do you think we could all go fishing together?

Subject:	Urgent need//Sr. Java/J2EE developer/Architect // Philadelphia, PA // 12
Sender:	Sudha
Date:	21.11.2011
Background:	Horatio licks his balls. Woof, woof.

Hi,

This is SUDHA ------- with ------INC, please do send me your updated resume with contact details if you are interested with any of the below positions by mentioning the position number ASAP To know more about us, please visit www.------inc.com

[job details]

Thanks & Regards

Sudha -----

----- Inc.

Atlanta, Georgia 30328

Direct: (678) --- ----

Phone: (678) --- ----

Thank you Sudha - when will this position be available?

Hi,

Once I submit your profile I can tell you regarding this.

Thanks & Regards

Sudha

Ok, let me know after you've done this. I'll walk the dog and check back with you.

For this I requirement some information with your updated resume ASAP:

Legal Name:

Current location:

Best number to reach you:

Total IT Exp (Yr):

Java Exp (Yr):

Work authorization/ Visa status:
Thanks & Regards
Sudha

I just returned with Horacio (my Scottish Deerhound). He's so big, sometimes I wonder who's walking who. Anyway, I got your form and I have just one reservation - in the past, after providing this type of information, I started to get 'girlie' magazines in the mail. Do you protect this information and if yes, how so?

OK,I can put it confidential until unless you confirm the pay for this position, if you are scared to provide this information in mail, please provide your contact number so that I will call you and we can have a conversation.
Thanks & Regards
Sudha

Sudha, what is the rate range so I can confirm the pay. Also, here is a picture of my dog:

{sent a link to a very good-looking Scottish Deerhound}

Around $53/ hr on W2.
Thanks & Regards
Sudha

Just to confirm, I don't look at the 'girlie' magazines - I just give them to Horacio (he likes to look at the pictures while he licks his balls). Is there any official document that I need to approve, or simply confirm the rate via email?

Anthony,
I am just trying to reach at 631.---.----.
Confirmation will be taken after the discussion on call.
So let me know the best time to reach you on call.
Thanks & Regards
Sudha

Yes Sudha, definitely call me when I am home. I am going to give Horacio a bath - actually, what I do is fill the tub half-way, turn on the shower, and we both get in. He uses a different shampoo than I. Is there anything I need to prepare for our conversation?

No preparation required and I also want to know that are you ok with the rate part? ($53/hr on W2)
Thanks & Regards
Sudha

Would you be able to do a bit better on the rate if it was corp-to-corp? Me and Horacio have our own company, WWBLC Inc. (Woof-Woof Ball-Lickers Consulting).

If it was on corp - corp rate will be up to $60/hr but the payment terms are Payment Terms would be monthly invoicing and net 30.
Thanks & Regards
Sudha

I apologize - Horatio does not understand this. Woof.

I am talking about job opening for you!
Thanks & Regards
Sudha

Thank you very much Sudha. What are the next steps? Woof. Woof.

Whats this means Woof. Woof?
And I can forward your profile once I talk to you only.
Thanks & Regards
Sudha

Oh, that's just a Scottish-Deerhound endearment.

I don't recall if we had spoke before the ball-licking.
Please let me know.

Until unless I talk to you and getting any information from you I cant submit your profile.
Thanks & Regards
Sudha

Ok. I'll call you tomorrow after I shave Horatio's sack.
What number can you be reached at?
Woof. Woof.

Subject:	Urgent need//Sr. Java/J2EE developer/Architect // Philadelphia, PA // 12
Sender:	Sudha
Date:	21.11.2011
Background:	Do you like my profile?

TITLE:JAVA DEVELOPER
LOCATION; KETTERING, OH
DURATION:FULL TIME
[job details]
Looking forward to working with you...
With Regards,
Srini -----
Sr. Manager
------------, Inc
Phone: (732) --- ----

Srini,
This looks very challenging - I am interesting!
Anthony

Hi Anthony,
Please do send me your profile....
Looking forward to working with you...
With Regards,
Srini

Srini,
I have attached a profile of myself.

{attached a picture of some guy in a suit}

Anthony can you please do send me your resume ......?
Looking forward to working with you...
With Regards,

Actually Srini, I am quite relieved - I thought you were going to ask for nudies of me (like the last place). Anyway, let me rework my resume and I'll email it to you. Is there anything specific I should highlight?

Nothing
Looking forward to working with you...
With Regards,
Srini

The reason I ask is because the last guy wanted to know my sexual orientation, waist size, favorite positions, etc. I was a bit reluctant to send this information, but at least didn't send him the nudies. Do you want the document in doc or pdf format?

Word document
Looking forward to working with you...
With Regards,

Thank you Srini, at least I know you're for real. This other guy was talking about 'dirty sanchez', 'dog in a bathtub', 'rusty trombone', and other references that I did not understand. The education portion of my resume is incomplete - should I finish this before I send it?

Subject:	Urgent need//Sr. Java/J2EE developer/Architect // Philadelphia, PA // 12
Sender:	Lateef (Rick)
Date:	21.11.2011
Background:	Ok, but don't let my mom find out!

GREETINGS...!!
Java/IBM Sterling CPQ Designer and Developer, Location:PA
Design and develop Sterling CPQ (Configure Price Quote) for
(MSO/Telco)s pre-sales commercial business unit.
[job details]
Thanks & Regards,
Rick
Technical Recruiter
----- Technologies Inc
Dallas, TX 75287
Direct : (972) --- ----

Lateef,
I am interesting! By when would you need a copy of my
resume?
Thanks.

That's Fine..!! Can you please let me have your Resume and
current location With a your visa status So that I can call you
and we can discuss more on this...!
Thanks & Regards,
Rick

I am having my mom mail my resume to you immediately - it
should arrive this week.
Thank you.

Send me your contact number I will do call you
Thanks & Regards,
Rick

My mom won't let me use the phone, but when she goes out for her therapy, I'll sneak back onto the computer and we can skype– sound ok?

I am still waiting for your reply can you do it ASAP so that I can go ahead with submission
Thanks & Regards,
Rick

Lateef,
Listen, I'm in a bit of trouble over here and have to finish cleaning my room - would it be ok if my mom called you to discuss? She knows all of my educational and work history. Where can she reach you?

Afterword / Epilogue

Since I started writing this book, I have accepted a fulltime job with a wonderful company, and am surrounded by professional, interesting people. Lucky me, since I have pissed off so many recruiters, I have very few resources to utilize if I should ever need to find another job.

In future writings, I will go much deeper undercover (I will use a different email address). Additionally, I will explore with you some of the most highly-skilled communication and behavioral examples (I will use even more profanities and curse word phrases).

I sincerely hope you enjoyed reading this book, and would love to hear of your experiences as you apply the many techniques described in this book. Please send your emails to me at getthatjob@gofurthercorp.com, but be careful – I might reply!

Made in the USA
Charleston, SC
08 June 2012